The Satisfied Patient:
A Guide to Preventing Malpractice Claims by Providing Excellent Customer Service

James W. Saxton, Esq.

The Satisfied Patient: A Guide to Preventing Malpractice Claims by Providing Excellent Customer Service is published by HCPro Inc.

Copyright 2003 HCPro Inc.   5   4   3   2

IISBN I-57839-270-5

James W. Saxton, Esq., Author
Dale Seamans, Executive Editor
Wendy Johnson, Managing Editor
Leah Tracosas, Copy Editor
Jean St. Pierre, Creative Director
Tom Philbrook, Cover Designer
Mike Mirabello, Senior Graphic Artist
Matthew Sharpe, Graphic Artist
Suzanne Perney, Executive Publisher
Sally Saxton, Cartoonist

Advice given is general. Readers should consult professional counsel for specific legal, ethical, or clinical questions. Arrangements can be made for quantity discounts.

For more information, contact:

HCPro Inc.
200 Hoods Lane
Marblehead, MA 01945
Telephone: 800/650-6787 or 781/639-1872
Fax: 781/639-2982
E-mail: *customerservice@hcpro.com*

Visit HCPro Inc. and the Greeley Company at
www.hcmarketplace.com* and *www.greeley.com   17935

Contents

Acknowledgements

My thanks goes out to the many physicians, hospital risk managers, executives, nursing home administrators, and other health care professionals with whom I have had the pleasure to work. They are hard-working, dedicated, and have provided me with invaluable experience. I am privileged to work alongside them. I also have appreciated the efforts of the editorial staff at HCPro, including Dale Seamans and Wendy Johnson. Thanks also to my talented wife Sally, who drew the cartoons included in this book. I have received much support from my entire family. In addition, Maggie Finkelstein, an attorney at Stevens & Lee, provided invaluable assistance with researching information for many of the chapters. Stevens & Lee has been a strong supporter of my work over the years. Time and again, they have shown their strong commitment to the healthcare industry.

About the Author

James W. Saxton, Esq.

James W. Saxton is a shareholder with the law firm of Stevens & Lee, where he is chair of the firm's health care litigation group and co-chair of the firm's health law group. Stevens & Lee has a full-service health law practice, representing health care clients throughout the country on multiple business, regulatory, and litigation issues.

Saxton specializes in creating customized risk management and risk engineering loss-control systems for health care organizations, and represents health care professionals in litigation claims. He speaks nationally on the subject of medical malpractice and liability risk reduction, and regularly presents educational programs for the entire spectrum of health care professions. He has created educational videos and handbooks, participated in national teleconferences, published more than 100 articles, co-authored two text books, and writes the free weekly e-zine, *Liability Reduction Connection,* published and distributed by HCPro Inc., Marblehead, MA.

Saxton is chair of the American Health Lawyers Association's Practice Group on Healthcare Liability and Litigation and a member of the Pennsylvania Bar Association, American Bar Association, and past president of the Hansel Brown Inn of Courts.

The Satisfied Patient: A Guide to Preventing Malpractice Claims by Providing Excellent Customer Servce, represents more than 20 years of experience working with health care professionals on risk management and litigation issues, inside and outside of the courtroom.

Introduction

Although there has always been the cloud of a potential malpractice case looming above health care professionals, no one ever suspected that it would have such a dramatic effect on physician practices, hospitals, nursing homes, or the community at large. It has arguably hindered access to care in many areas of the country. In 2002, this threat caused a number of hospital programs to close and physicians to either limit their practice areas or retire altogether.

For individual physicians, it is no longer business as usual. A few malpractice claims can mean exorbitant professional liability insurance premiums, or even the unavailability of insurance. The drastic increase in severe verdicts means that in certain cases a defendant's assets are at risk just by entering the courtroom.

Too often, the concepts of satisfaction, service, and communication are seen as "soft" or nonessential. It is time for a change. Legislation has helped in some jurisdictions, but more is needed at the state and federal levels. Risk managers' responsibilities have doubled amid the regulatory requirements of such legislation as the Health Insurance Portability and Accountability Act of 1996 and the Emergency Medical Treatment and Labor Act. We must reevaluate how caregivers manage their liability risks.

The good news is that we now have more insight into why patients file malpractice claims and why juries sometimes award large sums to plaintiffs. We must use this information to reduce the likelihood that a claim will be filed in the first place and, if pursued, to strengthen our defense against it. The materials you'll find here will allow you to begin this important work today.

This book is therefore a jumping-off point to a new level of risk engineering and loss control. In these pages, you'll learn why patients file malpractice cases and how you can make an impact at every stage of a lawsuit. Once you know the causes, you will understand why certain strategies are effective risk management tools. You'll find out how to create an environment in which patients are less likely to sue if an adverse event does occur. You'll also learn the anatomy of a malpractice lawsuit, the vulnerable areas in health care delivery that plaintiffs' attorneys try to exploit, and how you can strengthen those areas within your organization.

This book is the culmination of more than 20 years of legal experience working with physicians, nurses, and other health care professionals, both within their practice settings and in the courtroom. Being in the courtroom and seeing how these principles impact a trial is invaluable. I have reviewed much of the literature on the subject, spoken with physician leaders and hospital chief executives, and compiled that information here in a practical form to aid in your liability risk reduction efforts.

These materials are meant as suggestions only. They are in no way a substitute for competent legal advice from a knowledgeable health care attorney. And because laws concerning confidentiality, informed consent, and patient abandonment can vary from state to state, or even from jurisdiction to jurisdiction, it is important that you consult with an attorney who is familiar with your state and local laws. Many of the proactive principles discussed in this book do apply across the board, however, and have helped many practices, hospitals, and retirement communities across the country brace themselves against the litigious environment we face. And although the physician will be

Introduction

the example in most of these materials, the principles described transcend multiple areas of health care delivery.

Finally, no introduction to this topic would be complete without mentioning how bright, driven, and extraordinarily hard working our health care professionals are. Although I will use examples of poor service or communication in this book to illustrate certain points, they by no means reflect the profession as a whole. However, if certain examples hit too close to home, I apologize but encourage you to learn from them.

—James W. Saxton, Esq.

The Problem

"We begin by slowly stirring in the initial ingredients for Patient Satisfaction."

Malpractice claims continue to rise, with plaintiffs winning more cases that go to trial than they did five years ago. Malpractice insurance premiums have also risen sharply in at least 18 states, hitting hospitals the hardest in the high-risk areas of obstetrics, emergency care, neurosurgery, trauma, and primary and preventive care, according to the American Medical Association.

Further, the costs of settling a case and the dollar amounts awarded in verdicts have doubled over the last five years. The rapid increase in severity, an inadequate premium base, and a downturn in investment income have made liability insurance premiums cost-prohibitive in some areas. In addition, the events of September 11, 2001, added to an already unstable excess insurance market. In many areas of the country, insurance became almost unavailable, forcing physicians into expensive state-run programs.

Hospitals located in states with rising medical malpractice insurance premiums are struggling to adapt, according to the American Hospital Association. Consider the following statistics:

- 53% of hospitals say recruiting physicians has become more difficult

- 45% of hospitals report a loss of, or reduced coverage in, the emergency department

- 19% report a significant impact on access to care in the local community

Meanwhile, verdict awards have continued to escalate. According to discussions with jurors and national malpractice insurance experts, here are some reasons why:

1. **Patient expectations are at an all-time high.** Health care marketing boasts service, quality, and success. The Internet allows patients to learn about the wonderful advances in medicine, so many consumers expect to be diagnosed and cured quickly, painlessly, and cheaply. The public has come to believe that if they can get to a physician, an emergency department, or a hospital, they can be healed regardless of the stage of their illness. If they are in a hospital, many patients believe they are absolutely "safe." Of course, this is what we all want to believe—but this isn't reality. When unfortunate results occur, patients sometimes look for someone to blame.

2. **Rising health care costs create ready-made resentment in patients.** As health care costs rise, patients expect more for their money. When they don't receive the care they expect, they may feel cheated and become resentful. Consider the following example from a deposition:

    Every time I visit Mom at the hospital, I try to tell the nurses she needs to be watched more carefully. When I'm there, I almost never see a nurse. And a physician? Forget it. I know they're blowing me off. I have almost gotten into arguments with them about the side rails on the bed. They tell me that they don't need to be up. I tell them I have known my mom for 52 years and I know they need to be up. Now, not surprising to me, I get a sheepish call from the hospital to tell me that Mom has fallen, but they think she's okay. I'm not surprised—I knew this would happen.

    There is a lot going on in this example. Although the patient's family member appears critical, the nurse probably could have communicated better by explaining why the side rails should be down.

3. **Reimbursement is shrinking.** This is a very significant problem. Operational costs are increasing, reimbursement is decreasing, and payers are demanding the same level of quality that health care professionals have always provided. These factors place more stress on caregivers who already feel stretched thin.

4. **Society mistrusts health care professionals.** The public has been deluged with information about health care, and unfortunately much of it has been negative. For example, a general surgeon recalled how he received a phone call from a local medical malpractice plaintiff's attorney who wanted to use the surgeon as an expert witness for a case he

might file. He told the surgeon that a patient was sitting in his office and appeared to be suffering severe complications. The patient had undergone outpatient surgery two days earlier. The attorney said the patient looked extremely pale and weak, had a fever, and could not walk without assistance. The surgeon told the attorney to call an ambulance immediately!

The implications of this story are shocking. Ambulatory surgery centers are excellent about postoperative instructions, and there is little doubt that the patient was provided with his physician's telephone number in case any complications occurred. Instead, the patient chose to visit a medical malpractice attorney for answers to his questions.

5. **Plaintiff's attorneys are aggressive.** Prosecuting medical malpractice cases continues to be big business. Billboards urge disgruntled patients to "assert their rights." Television ads run in the middle of the workday, seemingly targeted at people who may be out of work due to an injury. Personal injury attorneys pack phonebooks with ads.

   Of course, there are many fine plaintiffs' attorneys who appropriately steer their clients away from litigation if the case has no merit. In fact, about 70% of claims nationally are closed without payment.

6. **Expert witnesses complicate matters.** Testimony from expert witnesses is required in all but the simplest cases, where the doctrine of *res ipsa loquitur*—a Latin term meaning, "the thing speaks for itself"— applies, i.e., the wrong limb was operated on. But this has not turned out to be a very significant screening goal. Defense counsels have heard experts testify on behalf of plaintiffs that any miss on a radiograph or postoperative infection is evidence of malpractice. Sometimes experts do not receive all of the necessary information to provide a truly

informed opinion. Some jurisdictions have passed legislation in an effort to establish some standards. A few professional societies also have their own standards in place.

7. **The legal system's checks and balances seem to be askew.**
   Multimillion dollar verdicts account for one out of every four jury verdicts, although the transactional costs associated with a trial (i.e., attorneys, experts, litigation costs, etc.) can eat up more than 50% of any verdict or settlement. Without caps on damages, as is still the case in many jurisdictions, there exists the potential of a highly emotional verdict by a jury that is swayed by a skilled plaintiff's attorney's case.

A close analysis of these problems helps us understand why putting proactive principles into place is imperative. Expectations will not change on their own, but we can influence whether patients seek an attorney and, if they do, whether they'll be able to put a strong case together. We can do something about the evidence a jury may ultimately see and hear. Understanding the problems will lead us to solutions.

Reporting requirements

Chapter One

One example of how important patient satisfaction has become: The Centers for Medicare & Medicaid Services (CMS) has considered mandatory public disclosure of patient satisfaction surveys in order for hospitals to receive Medicare rembursement. The agency for Healthcare Research and Quality is working with CMS to develop a standard survey. CMS wants to make the results available to Medicare beneficiaries. (More information can be found at *www.ahrq.gov*). This information could also be used to decide for which managed care panels employers want to sign up. This wave is just beginning to break—and is leaving in its wake some very significant economic consequences. For now, however, particpation in the initiative is voluntary.

The National Practitioner Data Bank (NPDB) can also be considered a cost associated with medical malpractice claims. Created by the Health Care Quality Improvement Act of 1986, the NPDB requires hospitals and other entities to report any monetary payments a practitioner makes to resolve a malpractice claim. The information becomes part of a national computerized information clearinghouse that can be accessed by a medical staff services professional whenever a practitioner applies for staff privileges.

The general public does not have access to information in the NPDB, although national legislation to change this is occasionally proposed. Many states make their own malpractice-related information quasi public, however. Pennsylvania, for example, requires physicians to report all filed lawsuits to the state board of medicine. Consumer groups continue to push this trend.

Physicians must consider all of these costs carefully when deciding whether to settle a case. They should consider the implications of a report to the NPDB and, if applicable, to their state board of medicine. They should also consider how a settlement would impact their malpractice insurance and ability to be credentialed at area hospitals, health systems, and health plans.

Malpractice Claims Affect More Than Your Money

The cost of defending medical malpractice suits is increasing. Professional liability insurance is almost prohibitive in some areas of the country. Premiums for many physician specialties have doubled, and in some cases tripled, during recent years. Some physicians simply cannot find coverage unless they seek help in a state-funded program. Others restrict their practices, retire early, relocate their practice, or play the odds and go without insurance. Some hospitals have not been able to find coverage and at times have had to close certain services. As a result, hospitals and physicians are turning to alternative markets or self-funding their exposures.

The International Risk Management Institute says there is an "urgent" need for measures to reduce the soaring costs of medical malpractice insurance. It's no wonder: The American Medical Association recently surveyed 1,000 hospitals and found that 53% have difficulty recruiting physicians. About 45% said high medical liability insurance premiums have forced them to reduce their emergency department coverage, while nearly 35% report that high premiums have hurt their ability to provide trauma care and obstetrics services.

Of course, liability insurance isn't the only risk-related cost. Some costs are harder to quantify, such as the emotional impact that lawsuits have on the physician, medical staff, nurses, patients, and family members. The litigation process is long and cumbersome, and the trial itself can take several weeks or months. Documents must be reviewed and depositions taken—all of which can stir up a variety of emotions. It's not uncommon for defendants to develop physical symptoms when reviewing the status of a claim, reading a plaintiff's expert's reports, or reviewing what individual witnesses have said in their depositions. Your attorney will need you to review, analyze, and discuss all of these issues, notwithstanding that you would probably like to forget that the lawsuit has ever occurred.

Defendants also experience pain and suffering, since malpractice claims fly in the face of a health care professional's commitment to help others. To hear an assertion that one's caregiving has harmed or even killed someone is a traumatic blow, to say the least. Further, the litigation process can take years, and will resurface again and again, whenever the physician is recredentialed, applies for privileges at another organization or institution, or applies for a personal mortgage or loan.

Defendants must strike a delicate balance between following the twists and turns of their case and becoming preoccupied with it. Physicians should try to compartmentalize the case in their minds, placing it in a separate space so it doesn't not trouble them all the time. This is no easy task, especially if adverse local or national publicity enters the mix.

Staff and family

A malpractice case touches everyone: physicians, medical staff, nurses, patients, and family members. Staff may have to take time off from work to prepare for and provide a deposition. They may even have to act as a witness during trial. Often, tensions arise between the physician and staff over documentation that was or was not made, or a process that was or was not followed. The more stressful a case is for a caregiver, the more stressful it is for his or her staff. This tension is usually unspoken but clearly felt.

Sometimes physicians are reluctant to discuss the case with staff. And while discussions should be kept to a minimum due to confidentiality and strategic concerns, it is impossible to keep staff completely in the dark. In one situation, staff learned about a case against their physician from a newspaper! This is the wrong way to inform staff, as they will be unprepared to answer questions from patients and may feel offended for being kept in the dark. A little communication and reassurance can go a long way, especially if staff members are later called as witnesses.

Family members also feel the effects of a malpractice case. Trials are among the most stressful events in a person's life. It is very difficult for a family to go through a malpractice trial and come out unscathed. Family members may feel helpless or resentful that the case is stealing time and energy away from their loved one for a lengthy period of time. It hangs over the family and prevents them from breathing easy until the case is settled—which can sometimes take years. Support, therefore, is critical.

Chapter Two

Medical malpractice allegations can also have an unfortunate effect on the physician-patient relationship. Many physicians who have been sued start to view their patients as potential adversaries. They wonder, "Who is going to sue me next?"

Data actually supports this fear. A physician who has been sued once is more likely to be sued again than a physician who has never been sued. This may be caused by the negative change in the patient-physician relationship. One might assume that certain practices, such as documentation, would improve after a lawsuit has been filed. However, research data suggests the opposite, emphasizing the impact that a malpractice claim can have on the physician-patient relationship. This is why it is so important to make patients feel a sense of responsibility for their own treatment. (See Chapter Six: Patient Involvement and Accountability, p. 45.) Never let relationships with patients become adversarial.

How many claims are too many?

A few years ago, it was perfectly acceptable for a busy practitioner to have several malpractice claims. Today, the acceptable threshold for malpractice claims is much different and can limit your practice.

So-called "corporate negligence theories" have grown dramatically across the country based, in part, on the premise that organizations must ensure patient safety through a very carefully developed and carried out credentialing process. As a result, hospitals, health plans, and other organizations are requesting more information about individual claims. Some managed care organizations won't even consider a provider for a medical panel if he or she has more than three claims.

Hospitals are also looking more closely at their credentialing criteria. Some delve deeper into a caregiver's abilities if the caregiver has multiple malpractice claims. They may ask questions about the caregiver's documentation patterns and communication skills.

When you consider all of the costs associated with a medical malpractice case, you'll find that it is clearly worth the time, expense, and resources to determine how to stop a lawsuit from being filed in the first place. And you can; these claims are preventable.

KEY

CONSIDER THE CONSEQUENCES OF NOT TAKING CERTAIN RISK MANAGEMENT PRINCIPLES TO THE NEXT LEVEL. NEARLY 70% OF ALL CLAIMS ARE PREVENTABLE AND 100% OF CLAIMS WILL BE EASIER TO MANAGE DURING THE TRIAL IF PROACTIVE RISK MANAGEMENT PRINCIPLES ARE INCORPORATED UP FRONT.

What Causes Malpractice Claims?

To truly understand how certain proactive risk management principles can help reduce claims, first examine the causes of malpractice claims. There are several factors that make a patient likely to seek an attorney. A patient who leaves your office or practice with unmet expectations, for example, is more likely to sue. And we know that it is not always easy to meet all of their expectations. Lower reimbursement—or, at times, a lack of it—makes it more difficult to provide a high level of service and responsiveness. It is therefore important to learn how to provide good service in a cost-efficient manner.

Gerald Hickson, MD, associate dean for clinical affairs and director of the Vanderbilt Center for Patient and Professional Advocacy, has researched and analyzed the course of professional liability issues for many years, and was kind enough to discuss his work with us.

He is convinced that we can reduce liability risk through education, a better understanding of what causes a claim in the first place, and doing a better job of sharing data with physicians.

Based on his many decades of research in this area, including a recently published work in the June 2002 *Journal of the American Medical Association*, Hickson describes three broad categories that promote professional liability claims. The first category comprises, simply, individuals whose personalities and communication skills make it more difficult for patients to truly hear and understand them. It is critical for this type of physician to be aware of and try to improve this behavior. Such improvement requires an awareness of the problem—through physician data collected by organizations such as hospitals or insurers. Next, appropriate education and training has to occur. Both steps are easier said than done.

The second category involves the general health care system and the situations it presents that increase risk exposure. These include physicians who work too many long hours, and staff who are not helpful or cognitive of important service and communication issues.

In the third category are physicians who exhibit poor behavior or poor communication skills. Physicians are human, after all, and are prone to less than ideal behavior from time to time. Hickson points out that many times these physicians simply aren't reminded of what is or is not acceptable behavior under particular circumstances. Patients are perhaps too tolerant and should report to physicians when disagreeable behavior occurs.

While good communication is important, Hickson also notes that it takes more than a physician's attendance at a seminar or course to improve behavior or the system. Health care providers have to help each other and look at comparative data to understand what is or is not acceptable. Physicians need tools to effect change, including proper motivation.

KEY

A LACK OF COMMUNICATION OR PERSONAL CONNECTION WITH PATIENTS NOT ONLY EFFECTS THE FREQUENCY OF CLAIMS, BUT ALSO THE SEVERITY. A COMBINATION OF MALPRACTICE AND A SERVICE LAPSE CAN LEAD TO LAWSUITS AND EXTRAORDINARY VERDICTS.

Service lapses make claims harder to defend

A renowned plaintiff's attorney once told a story during a national conference. This lawyer was one of several legal experts on a panel trying to help an audience of insurance executives understand why jury awards in malpractice trials were rising so high. He began to explain that seven-, eight- and sometimes nine-figure verdicts were often justified. The audience did not accept this explanation and pushed him for a more accurate account of why the severity of jury verdicts was increasing. The audience figured he must know since he and his firm had accomplished this result time and time again.

After a great deal of backpedaling, the lawyer set forth his conclusions. He explained that his firm had ceased pursuing medical malpractice claims a few years ago. This statement was quite surprising since his firm was well known for concentrating on such claims. He went on to explain that the firm received many calls from patients who felt malpractice had occurred. He and his colleagues would listen, evaluate, and have appropriate experts review the care. Often it appeared to be a bona fide claim of malpractice.

However, appearances weren't enough. The firm wanted evidence of some type of service lapse—e.g., a miscommunication, lack of disclosure about a complication, or even rudeness. Juries can relate to such missteps and might be more willing to award substantial verdicts against them. They are also harder for providers to defend.

Chapter Three

Your first line of defense: Communication and service

The first opportunity to prevent a case is to evaluate the "macro"—or cultural environment—of your practice. Is it geared toward providing truly superior service and excellence to your patients? (See Chapter Five: Becoming a Five Star Service Provider, p. 33.)

Patients seek attorneys in the first place due to lack of information. They may experience an undesirable result and want to know why, but their physician doesn't return their calls. Or they may already have a poor relationship with their physician and then experience a poor clinical result. The communication that takes place following the poor result will drive what the patient does next, as well as become part of the plaintiff attorney's evaluation and evidence. If you have created a positive environment and relationship with the patient, he or she will be more likely to seek answers from you than an attorney when problems occur.

Next, analyze your micro—or day-to-day—environment by examining your service at the operational level. A microanalysis digs down to the root causes of a malpractice claim. What kind of relationship does your office or department create with patients? Does the receptionist say hello and make eye contact when patients enter? When the physician is ready to see a patient, does a nurse simply bark his or her name out, turn around, and walk down the hall, expecting the patient to follow? Is the patient's appointment rushed due to the physician's hectic schedule?

The following are some classic examples culled from real scenarios of poor physician-patient relationships that clearly illustrate how excellent service principles and strong communication skills are your first line of defense against a malpractice claim:

- **The patient experiences an excessive wait without explanation or apology.** There is a cumulative effect to waiting that is problematic—patients wait to schedule a visit, wait in the reception area when they arrive for the visit, and wait in the exam room. Chronic waiting is used by trail lawyers to suggest both a lack of organization and respect for your patients. Moreover, plaintiffs' attorneys like to show how long waits are symptomatic of a disorganized and hurried physician.

- **The patient doesn't feel respected.** Does the physician communicate in a way that appears judgmental? Does he or she fail to make eye contact, interrupt the patient, or appear to take the patient's symptoms lightly? A disgruntled or hurt patient never forgets this.

- **The physician is not available to discuss complications that may occur.** A patient calls his or her surgeon with questions about medication or post-surgical symptoms. The physician has moved on to the next scheduled procedure and doesn't return the call. Questions go unanswered. Family members come to the hospital looking for the physician and fail to understand why he or she is not available. This is both a major source of litigation and can be a significant detriment to your future defense. Disclosure issues are a hot button for severe claims awards.

- **Important information is never communicated to the family.** The physician scheduled to perform the surgery is unable to do so and substitutes a colleague at the last minute. The family is not informed. A complication occurs and the patient dies. When the new surgeon approaches the family to inform them, their first question is, "Who are you?" Anger and mistrust ensue.

- **The physician offers only vague, nonanswers.** A surgeon approaches a family following a surgical complication and says, "I have no idea what happened, nor will I ever." The family obtains counsel to get to the facts.

- **Informed consent is obtained, but the nervous patient doesn't truly understand everything discussed.** The patient is so anxious while the physician explains his or her procedure that the patient doesn't really hear everything that was said. The patient calls the physician's office the next day with questions, but office staff don't have time to walk the patient through all of the information again. The patient's questions aren't answered and he or she becomes angry when a complication occurs. In court, the plaintiff's attorney describes how the patient was denied important information and instructions.

- **The physician talks down to the patient.** During a telephone conversation with a new mother, a pediatrician explains with a flat tone, "I get these calls from new parents all the time. I know its hard but you'll simply have to get used to your baby's crying. We saw him two days ago, and he appeared fine. Call us if there is a change, such as a fever or different symptoms." The mother feels chided and embarrassed by the physician's remarks and does not call back when the baby's symptoms worsen. Several days later, the same woman brings her dehydrated, feverish infant to the emergency department, where the baby has a seizure.

Common threads throughout each of these scenarios include a lack of communication, miscommunication, lack of service excellence in the patient-physician relationship, and a feeling of abandonment. These threads can prompt a disgruntled patient to seek an attorney, make the attorney more willing to take the case, and make the jury more sympathetic to the plaintiff.

Incorporating true service excellence principles into your practice and creating a culture in which communication skills are a premium are your first defenses against a claim. These actions help create a mutually respectful relationship with the patient that prevents feelings of mistrust or anger.

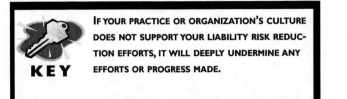

KEY

IF YOUR PRACTICE OR ORGANIZATION'S CULTURE DOES NOT SUPPORT YOUR LIABILITY RISK REDUCTION EFFORTS, IT WILL DEEPLY UNDERMINE ANY EFFORTS OR PROGRESS MADE.

Second line of defense: Make your case less appealing to a plaintiff's attorney

Medical malpractice attorneys are businesspeople who evaluate the economic value of each case. A patient who suffers an adverse event but who gives your office or facility a thumbs-up for good service is not a good investment from a malpractice attorney's point of view: It wouldn't play out well in the courtroom.

Consider the following experience related by a plaintiff's attorney. A family came to her with a complaint about the nursing home where their mother died due to complications from an infection. Nursing home staff had acknowledged that they erred by not reporting the mother's condition to her physician in time and that the responsible parties had been terminated. The family was appreciative of the nursing home's honesty, but sued because they wanted to make sure the same thing didn't happen to someone else. They told the attorney that their mother's care had otherwise been fine.

The attorney asked the family what they hoped to gain from the lawsuit. They explained that they wanted the nursing home to forgive some unpaid expenses and to ensure that the error would never be repeated. The attorney decided not to press forward with a lawsuit and instead advised the family to contact the nursing home to discuss their concerns.

Third line of defense: Good customer service

To be competitive, you must embrace a strong service component. Hospitals, medical groups, and other health care facilities are placing more emphasis on their roles as hospitality providers who strive to provide top service while encouraging patient involvement and accountability. This trend is fueled in part by the knowledge that service excellence can significantly reduce liability exposure. It also is driven by economics. Facilities or practices that truly provide excellent customer service will obtain greater market share as they attract more patients and payers to their services.

Sophisticated patient satisfaction surveys can be taken and tallied via the Internet, allowing employers, payers, and the consumer to quickly view results. These results are becoming increasingly important to payers. Pilot programs in which third-party payers offer bonuses to physicians who generate high marks on patient satisfaction surveys are sprouting up across the country, including one by the Centers for Medicare & Medicaid Services.

As reviewed in previous chapters, the costs of a professional liability claim are high and varied. But there are strategies available to reduce them while enhancing your customer service component. The above are just a few examples.

The Right Environment:
One small change can turn things around

One practice was experiencing significant waits, particularly on Mondays, when they were more likely to have many "add-ons" after the weekend. Patient visits would back up, creating an annoyance for patients and stress for the whole office. Because the entire practice ran late on those days, staff stayed until late in the evening. They received overtime pay, but were still upset because their plans with their families or other obligations were disrupted. Nurses and other staff began to resent the physicians, who in turn began to feel a lack of respect from their staff. As a result, the practice lost some good, long-time employees.

Consequently, new employees had to be hired and trained—only to have the whole cycle repeat. This created a significant administrative expense. It also left patients feeling rushed and disrespected, and staff and physicians feeling stressed. This, as you can imagine, is a risky combination.

Finally, someone suggested that the practice leave small holes in the schedule for unanticipated needs that may arise, especially during peak times. In addition, all staff were taught how to show empathy for patients annoyed by a long wait and apologize promptly for any delays. The practice also posted the following notice in the waiting area:

We are sorry! We always try to meet your scheduled appointment time. Sometimes we run late and we apologize. A patient's visit sometimes takes longer than we anticipate. Sometimes that patient is you! Thanks for your patience.

The results were astounding. Physicians and staff began working together more productively and profitably, and patients felt better about their care. Although the practice initially feared that they would lose money due to the holes in their schedule, they found that the holes were constantly filled. In fact, they saved money by not requiring as much overtime. Most significantly, staff were less tense and more productive. The schism between physicians and staff was mended. Again, it is all about creating the right environment.

Creating a Caring Environment

A lot of work goes into creating the right environment—it is not solely the physician's job. Good patient satisfaction begins with the environment that exists in your office, clinic, hospital, or organization. The environment has a strong bearing on whether the patient will seek an attorney and, equally important, whether the attorney will take the case. It also affects the settlement value and how the judge and jury will consider the case.

The "environment" extends far beyond interactions between the patient and the physician, nurse, or other health care professional. In fact, it begins long before such interactions take place. Consider the following:

- **Marketing:** How do patients find you? What information do you send to them before their first visit? How easy do you make their first visit (i.e., scheduling, directions, parking, etc.)?

- **Telephone etiquette:** Does the receptionist answer by immediately asking callers to "hold please," or does he or she say, "Hello, Dr. Smith's office, how may I help you?" Does your office or practice use an automated telephone system that is difficult to navigate? How are questions answered when patients call in with them?

- **Reception etiquette:** Does the receptionist look up from his or her desk and make eye contact with patients when they walk in? Is the amount of time that patients spend in the reception area reasonable? Are the checkout and reception areas pleasant and easy to navigate? Is someone available to answer any last minute questions patients may have? Does an intake person ask patients to provide personal information, such as Social Security numbers, within earshot of other patients? What are patients able to overhear about other patients? (Many practices place a television opposite the reception area in an effort to draw patients' attention away from the reception area and to provide some ambient noise for confidentiality purposes.)

- **Tone versus time:** Does the physician appear frantic and rushed? Does he or she make eye contact with patients, ask open-ended questions, and allow patients time to answer questions without interrupting? (Studies show that an interruption occurs after an average of 25 seconds.)

- **Complaints:** Are complaints from patients or staff regarded as learning opportunities or nuisances? If there was a service lapse, do we still try to recover payment from the patient?

- **Staff morale:** Are there certain times during the day or certain days of the week when staff members are more likely to be pressed for time? Have staff received training and education about effective communication techniques? Do staff and physicians display a positive attitude?

Each of these areas comprises your overall environment. Reviewing them closely, you can begin to see how many opportunities you have to impress patients—either positively or negatively. It is important to examine all areas of patient interaction to identify your barriers to true service excellence and strategies for removing them.

Let's focus more closely on a few key areas of patient interaction:

Reception

When did you last spend time in your reception area? How crowded does it get? What do patients hear, see, and feel?

This area should be clean and organized. Provide comforts such as coffee, tea, or orange juice, and a separate children's area when appropriate. Current magazines and newspapers are helpful. Seating arrangements should prevent an inadvertent breach of confidentiality. In other words, try to keep patients busy, comfortable, and distracted from the fact that they are waiting.

Some practices have tried to turn the reception area into an educational area by providing stations where patients can watch educational videos or listen to audiotapes. Some provide private areas where patients can make phone calls. Others provide patients with a pager so they don't have to be confined to the waiting area while waiting for their appointment. Many of these ideas have come directly from patients who have completed patient feedback surveys.

> ✓ **Your reception area should positively market your practice at multiple levels.** Neil Baum, MD, a New Orleans urologist and author of several books about marketing physician practices, keeps a scrapbook filled with letters from patients in his reception area. Other practices have articles and newsworthy information on a bulletin board in the reception area (again, this is placed away from the front desk to encourage patients not to linger there). This information may interest your patients and take their mind off of a lengthy wait.

Long waits

The days when patients will settle for spending all day at the physician's office are no more. Chronic waits in excess of 45 minutes are no longer acceptable. In fact, there have been reports of patients actually billing physicians for their waiting time. Some patients have actually taken their physicians to small claims court because the physicians didn't pay the bill. In at least one instance, the magistrate ruled in favor of the patient.

An unexcused, unreasonable wait for which the patient does not receive an apology is a liability risk. Waits cause patients to slowly boil, especially long waits followed by rushed visits. It is little wonder that a patient would allege malpractice if there ever appeared to be a misdiagnosis. Consider the following deposition testimony:

> I had to get my sister to drop my daughter Annie off at preschool because I had an early appointment at my physician's office. This meant that I would owe my sister a favor forever, and boy did she remind me. I got there and waited over an hour and a half. It was early in the morning,

how could that possibly happen? I was watching my watch, I admit, because I had shopping to do, had to get to the post office, then had to pick Annie back up. It looked like none of it was going to get done. When I got in to see the physician, I could immediately tell she was having a bad day. She did not even look up at me. I actually felt sorry for her . . . I'm sure all the patients were giving her a hard time [but] she never even gave me an explanation. Then I had a world-record visit, which maybe was good because I had to pick Annie up, but I assumed she did at least everything she needed to do.

Later in the deposition:

Of course I told her about the lump in my breast. I went through the whole deal with her, but I'm not surprised she missed it that day. As I told you earlier . . .

It's time to attack wait times. To do so, you must first have an understanding of where you are. Do you know exactly how long your wait time is? A simple patient survey can reveal this information—and by benchmarking and reviewing it annually you'll recognize the problem areas you need to address.

Keep your eyes peeled while gathering data. One practice manager initiated such a survey to get a baseline on his office's average wait time. While tallying the results one day, he spied a physician literally erasing time on a timesheet so the physician's wait time would appear shorter. In the future, the manager might require his physicians to enter their information into the survey form with a black, felt-tipped pen.

Four ways to ease a long wait time

> **PLEASE**
>
> Let the receptionist know if you have been waiting for more than **15 minutes**

1. **Post signs:** Some practices post signs that urge patients to approach the reception desk if they wait more than 15 minutes. When the patient does approach the front desk, the well-trained receptionist apologizes and lets him or her know how much longer the wait may be. This simple interaction goes a long way toward cooling off any anger that may be simmering, since patients often become upset when they perceive that you don't care.

2. **Keep patients' expectations reasonable:** You can shape the patient's attitude about waiting by posting an appropriately worded statement in a patient brochure, on your Web site, and in the reception area. (See Chapter 3: What Causes Malpractice Claims?, p. 13.) This helps to diffuse some of the stress caused by the wait. It also shows that you are aware of it, respect the patient, and recognize that the patient's time is valuable.

3. **Keep patients informed:** In a surgical practice, let patients know ahead of time that the surgeon may be called away at the last minute helps. Offering an empathetic statement is useful. Certainly, offering time management strategies to physicians who seem to chronically run late can help, too. Above all, a sincere apology when physicians are running late is mandatory.

4. **Apologize:** Apologies can go a long way when done sincerely. Of course, the reverse is also true: Neglecting to apologize can have long lasting consequences. Apologizing sincerely means that the speaker is not looking down at the chart, writing a note, or mumbling the apology. It means that he or she is establishing eye contact, explaining why appointments are running late, and giving the patient the kind of attention and respect that you would expect if the same thing happened to you.

Telephone etiquette

Your office, practice, or facility is likely to receive a significant amount of calls from patients who need follow-up information to supplement a recent appointment. Not providing this information promptly to patients has significant clinical and patient satisfaction consequences.

Patients sometimes return home from an appointment and remember a burning question they forgot to ask or realize they were so nervous or preoccupied in the physician's office that they forgot everything the physician said. For example, if the physician appears to be rushed, and the patient has further questions, the patient may feel too intimidated to ask them.

Regardless of their cause, these telephone calls place tremendous stress on the practice. Most practices do not have the resources to repeat all of the information that patients received during the office visit. The physician is either with another patient or otherwise unavailable. The nurse may not be able to answer all of the patient's questions. Sometimes several days can lapse before the patient obtains the needed information and by then, it may not be timely. This harms patient care, is bad for patient satisfaction, and draws away from your resources.

It is also a major source of lawsuits. The information or instructions that the patient initially received was presumably very important. Perhaps it was not written down in detail in the patient's chart. The patient calls once, cannot reach the physician, and does not follow up. Days go by, the patient forgets about the information he or she needed and assumes everything will be fine. When something goes wrong, the patient blames the physician for not providing adequate instructions. Whether this turns into a claim could depend upon the quality of all information the patient received and how well it was documented.

Your practice or facility should have a system in place for responding to all patient inquiries. For example, a nurse or physician assistant might be responsible for answering general questions. Perhaps the physician will respond to specific clinical questions via e-mail. You may have a staff member call patients to let them know when they can expect to hear from the physician. You don't want patients sitting at home, waiting for the phone to ring.

Some practices have compiled a rather detailed set of instructions and answers to frequently asked questions for certain clinical circumstances, especially for certain procedures or issues that typically generate a high number of patient inquiries. They hand the information to patients and document it in the chart. This information exchange helps to boost patient satisfaction, provides them with written documentation regarding patient instructions, and reduces the number of telephone calls from patients.

The loop

The loop that is your office is an important yet often forgotten part of your overall environment. Walking the loop occasionally can provide you with a host of useful information and prevent you from becoming oblivious to your own environment. What, for example, do patients see, hear, and smell? Do employees sometimes leave the door to the break room open, allowing patients to overhear the employees' conversations with one another? Are there any disruptions along the loop, such as at billing or in a second waiting area? Is confidentiality maintained? Can patients inadvertently read information contained in the charts that hang outside exam room doors?

Tone

The tone your staff exhibit when summoning patients into the exam room is also important. Taking a few extra moments to smile, look the patient in the eye, and exchange a few friendly words can make a tremendous difference. Some patients have complained on patient satisfaction surveys that they feel "barked" at when called into the office. It does not take much energy to simply call out a patient's name in a friendly, softened tone. A smile and some light conversation can help. After all, patients are typically uncomfort-able, anxious, and apprehensive. Our job is to help them feel better.

Check out

The back end of the office—the part that takes care of billing, scheduling surgery, and insurance issues—is usually the business center. As such, the professionals who work there may not be as focused on the service and satisfaction components as the front-end staff. This must change. The individu-als who work in this area must be as service-oriented as the front-desk receptionist. Check-out staff are usually the last to interact with patients and are thus in a position to shape each patient's final impression of your practice or facility. Therefore, even the 30- or 60-second interactions that patients have with your check-out staff make all the difference in the world.

Check-out is where we see the results of our attempts to improve service. If we have provided clear and concise information during the visit—including complete written instructions, if necessary—we will need to spend less time with the patient upon check-out. Further, patients will be less likely to call back later with follow-up questions, will be more satisfied with their visit, more compliant, and less likely to sue if something has gone wrong.

Event management

An adverse event can have two different outcomes, depending on how it is handled. One outcome is a positive environment in which we help the patient and his or her family through the event; the other is a slew of allegations that we have tried to hide facts to protect ourselves from exposure.

Event management applies to every staff member in every setting. It means using service excellence and good communication when an adverse event does occur, having a process to investigate and disclose errors when appropriate, and recognizing a patient's changing needs when an event occurs. Event management does not simply happen: It requires training for the physician and staff on how to communicate and disclose medical errors to patients and their family members.

This is an area in which well-thought-out policies and procedures, together with an adequate amount of training, can make a big difference. It is also a hot button for the plaintiff's bar. When there is not adequate disclosure, the plaintiff's attorney will try to use any omissions as evidence of a cover-up. You can see how quickly it changes the entire dynamic.

KEY

A FRIENDLY, COMFORTABLE, AND RESPECTFUL ENVIRONMENT SETS A POSITIVE TONE WITH PATIENTS AND CAN MAKE THEM LESS LIKELY TO SUE. STAFF TURNOVER ALSO TENDS TO BE LESS, WHICH LEAVES YOU WITH A HAPPY, PRODUCTIVE, AND SEASONED STAFF. TRIAL LAWYERS SHY AWAY FROM BRINGING CASES AGAINST PRACTICES AND OFFICES THAT HAVE POSITIVE, HELPFUL ENVIRONMENTS BECAUSE THEY KNOW THAT JURORS ARE LESS LIKELY TO HAND OUT EXCESSIVE AWARDS AGAINST THEM.

Becoming a Five-Star Service Provider

Closely aligned with creating a caring environment is your ability to provide true service excellence. Achieving high rates of patient satisfaction—or more broadly put, customer satisfaction—can have powerful economic and business consequences, in addition to being one of the most prudent investments an organization can make toward accomplishing five-star status and ensuring the success of your health care organization. The organization that strives for this level of service will become the provider and the employer of choice.

Although this is not a new topic, there has been much focus on this area of health care delivery in recent years. There are often articles in contemporary health care magazines that describe how certain organizations strive for better patient satisfaction ratings and survey results.

Achieving patient satisfaction and providing excellent service may seem like common sense, but living it (i.e., smiling, being patient, not interrupting patients) on a daily basis can be extremely difficult. Does everyone in your organization answer phones in a way in which the caller feels respected, informed, and truly helped? Would all individuals within your organization go out of their way to help someone in the hallway who appears to be lost? When patients become frustrated, angry, and unreasonable, do your staff resist the urge to roll their eyes or sigh audibly? Have you given specific thought to true service excellence with regard to the way that your office is organized, such as its physical layout, documentation practices, and the ways in which employees are hired, trained, evaluated, and paid?

Becoming a five-star practice means focusing on patient satisfaction at both the macro (cultural) and micro (day-to-day operational) levels. When leaders at a health care organization say they truly embrace patient satisfaction as a cultural element, ask whether their staff have received training to sharpen their customer service and communication skills within the last calendar year. If the answer is no, they do not regard patient satisfaction seriously enough.

Customer service and communication will quickly decline if you do not pay attention to them. They must become woven into the very fabric of your organization. Top hospital chief executives around the country agree that this is a continuing process and that they are not where they would like to be. They never consider their jobs done and are always seeking opportunities to create a better experience for patients.

There is too often a tendency to approach this evaluation in a negative fashion. However, the focus should rather be on what we can do right than on what we are doing wrong.

We also need to reevaluate the meaning of true service excellence. True service excellence doesn't happen just because we want it to. It takes a top-down assessment to determine whether everyone in the organization is on the same cultural page.

Turning to the hospitality industry for inspiration

Have you ever considered modeling your patient satisfaction goals after some of the best customer service providers in the country, such as the Ritz-Carlton Hotel Company or the Walt Disney Company?

You might be thinking, "We are not a resort or a vacation spot, and this certainly isn't a place where you'll enjoy fine dining." But that misses the point.

True, a physician practice and a hospital are not resorts, nor do they offer fine dining (although some hospitals are striving to change this). However, the concept of treating the patient as one would a customer or hotel guest by trying to enhance his or her experience is critical to your success. Your efforts do not have to be fancy, fun, or exciting. But they should focus on identifying, meeting, and exceeding your patients' expectations. Strive to remove the barriers that prevent staff from providing five-star service. These are concepts very consistent with those embraced by the Ritz-Carlton Hotel Company and the Walt Disney Company. (See box on p. 39.)

We were privileged to spend some time discussing service excellence concepts with Robert George, corporate director of training and development for the Ritz-Carlton Hotel Company. He began his career at the company as a waiter and moved quickly through the ranks to his current position. Many of the company's leaders have also been promoted through the ranks and have a strong belief in its mission, which states, "The Ritz-Carlton Hotel is a place where the genuine care and comfort of our guests is our highest mission."

George summarizes the beginnings of the organization as a group of businesspeople who got together in the early 1980s and decided to develop the best hotels. They originally intended to build only eight hotels, but today they have more than 55, each known worldwide for their extraordinary service.

From the outset, they tried to ensure an unparalleled experience for all guests by paying painful attention to detail. Employees scour the hotel for service weaknesses so that they can correct them before they ever become apparent to guests—in other words, they work at continuous quality improvement.

The organization's goals are strikingly similar to those of hospital chief executives and physician leaders: The Ritz-Carlton Company does not merely want to satisfy its guests, but to make them loyal guests. To do this, one must personalize service, exceed expectations, and resolve problems quickly. And in this culture, employees are empowered to do so.

Its culture is pervasive. It begins with careful selection of employees. The company pays a competitive wage and hires individuals who will thrive in its culture. All candidates go through a rigorous interview process. When hiring, the company paints a realistic picture for its prospective employees, including the drive and discipline it requires. Although the tools for success are provided to employees, the Ritz-Carlton first makes sure the employee is a good fit.

George says that the most important feature to look for in prospective employees is their willingness to care. This is something you cannot train or teach, but must be developed through the culture. When your workers care, they energize one another. This becomes your first line of continuous quality improvement. Leaders, of course, lead by example and accomplish the same goal.

Ritz-Carlton employee training includes a mandatory orientation program on the first day of employment, followed by a mandatory check-up orientation 21 days later. At that time, the employees are asked, whether they have the tools and the work environment they need in order to provide top-notch service. George explains that this process is important because satisfied employees will perform their jobs well.

The result: Employees at the Ritz-Carlton are content with their jobs, which enables them to provide a high level of customer service. Astoundingly, Ritz-Carlton has a turnover rate that is below 25%, which is truly extraordinary for the hospitality industry.

Interestingly, in the late 1980s when it was considered the best of the best, then-Chief Operating Officer Horst Schulze, when asked where he felt the Ritz-Carlton fell on a scale of one to 10, indicated four—"the best of a lousy lot." Again, this illustrates the cultural challenge to continually determine how to wow the next guest and never sit back and congratulate yourself on a job well done.

In fact, Ritz-Carlton decided in the 1990 sto reinvent itself and work even harder to learn what its guests desired. A great deal of data collection and studies revealed that guests wanted to feel like they were being pampered at home. Specialists determined that guests wanted their needs to be anticipated. The guests wanted things done to make them comfortable without having to ask. Ritz-Carlton then became relentless in this effort.

How does the company motivate 25,000 employees to do this? It takes leadership and planning. Ritz-Carlton has worked hard to obtain and develop great leaders. Ten to 15 minutes before every shift, managers discuss relevant events, goals, and concerns with staff. If employees have any problems at the beginning of the day—including personal problems or barriers—the leaders try to reduce them to help employees provide true service excellence. This may be one of the most critical elements to their success: communicating with, and listening to, all employees.

Chapter Five

There is so much to learn from the Ritz-Carlton business model, and it is so consistent with those of other great service organizations worldwide. "Any organization can achieve excellence," George says. "The problem is that people end up with a focus on function rather than where their focus should be—on purpose."

Case Study: How Walt Disney
keeps customers satisfied

Another example of the commitment to and the benefits of striving for service excellence is evidenced by the Walt Disney Company, known for its outstanding customer service and clean, easy-to-use facilities. In reviewing literature such as *The Disney Way*, authored by Bill Capodagli and Lynn Jackson (1999, McGraw-Hill), it is apparent that we can learn from the service-excellence concepts practiced by the company and its Disney Institute, which offers seminars about Disney's brand of business management. As explained by Capodagli and Jackson, many of Disney's techniques for boosting customer satisfaction can be applied to health care organizations.

Innovative corporate culture practices existed at Disney from the beginning. Founder Walt Disney believed that every employee is the company and that every customer is a "guest." In this way, Disney's pleasant environment permeates throughout the entire organization, regardless of an employee's title or duties. Evidence of Disney's commitment to nurturing a cooperative corporate culture is reflected in its language. For example, Disney does not have employees; it has "cast members." They don't wear costumes; they don uniforms. They don't have jobs; they play "roles" in a show. These theatrical references reflect Disney's culture and help new "cast members" understand and appreciate its culture; while everyone may not know how to treat a customer, most people know how to treat a guest.

Disney's culture is grounded on three very important concepts: its heritage, an understanding of its day-to-day operations; and its vision. Day-to-day operation is the key to continuous improvement. It is recognized throughout the Disney culture that ultimately everyone is hired to create happiness for the guests.

There is a perception that an employer has to pay higher salaries and have better benefits than competitors in order to obtain a high level of service. However, these are not the only factors that motivate employees, as Disney has found. Non-monetary benefits, such as employee outings, can enhance the "cast" experience as well, and can make employees feel valued. Disney teaches its cast members to balance "quality cast experience, quality guest experience," and quality business practices.[1]

At Disney, and so many great service organizations, it is critical to hire the right person who will be the right fit. After all, it's more difficult to change someone's values, beliefs, and attitudes, than it is to enhance his or her technical skills. Hiring the right people to fit a job requires less time and effort to motivate them later on, makes them more productive. It can also result in fewer turnovers, providing tangible benefits to the bottom line. Disney has a turnover rate exceptionally below that normally seen in its industry. The theme-park industry generally averages 100% turnover. The rate in Walt Disney's theme parks stays below 30%.[2]

Industry leaders like Disney recognize that it is often a process that fails, not a person. Leaders of the organization must support employees by discovering why a process doesn't work and then take steps to fix it. At Disney, it's the leader's role to remove barriers that prevent cast members from delivering great service. They do this is by establishing a set of clear service standards and providing employees with a roadmap for decision-making.

There are other innovative ways in which world-class service organizations try to minimize the day-to-day frustrations that employees may encounter. For example, Disney has created policies for addressing virtually any kind situation imaginable: from helping guests who can't find their parked cars to fixing a customer's flat tire in the parking lot—a location which most companies would never hold up as a benchmark for quality service.

Disney has a high-percentage of repeat visitors, for which they strive to improve and enhance their experience. If you consistently perform at a very high service level, will your customer always expect more? And how do you continue to meet or exceed that expectation? Walt Disney believes that this can be accomplished by anticipating its guests' needs and meeting them promptly.

1 Capodagli, B. & Jackson, L. "The Disney Way." (1999).
2 Id.

Where to begin

Improving your service does not have to be an overwhelming endeavor. It can begin with a mission or plan for how you will educate your staff. The most important thing is getting started. Consider the following as jumping-off points:

✔ *Education and training*

One way to develop and continue this culture is through education and ongoing training. Everyone from the business manager to the receptionist to the housekeeping staff must understand how to communicate with each other and with patients, and what a service excellence culture means. It means exhibiting friendliness and helpfulness—even on the rainy Monday morning after a trying weekend. It means looking for opportunities to catch that service lapse before it reaches the customer. It also means striving to create not just patient satisfaction, but loyalty as well.

A kick-off training program should occur, but you also should offer ongoing inservices on difficult service issues. Professionally videotape such programs so that new employees can view them. Provide training on how to diffuse an angry patient, cultivate a loyal customer, effectively triage in a service-oriented fashion, and read and use body language. These are the types of tools that staff need but generally are not taught in many orientation programs.

When should you offer the programs? Health care organizations do not have the luxury of closing down so everyone can attend a program, so from a more pragmatic standpoint, several programs scheduled at different times may be more a reasonable alternative. Or as mentioned above, videotaping the program allows employees who cannot attend the program to view it at a later time.

After training takes place, the organization must strive to keep the new culture alive. That means making the concepts embraced by the organization part of the hiring process, orientation, individual evaluations, and the bonus structure. Leaders should always look for other opportunities to keep the culture alive, such as implementing an employee satisfaction program, employee suggestion box, employee-of-the-month program, and positive feedback from managers or physicians. Tremendous service organizations know they cannot accomplish true service excellence without high employee satisfaction. The two go hand-in-hand.

✔ *Identify and correct weaknesses*

Look for areas that need attention. For example, analyzing near-misses to prevent the same service lapse in the future is essential. Near-misses provide a laboratory in which we can discover what caused them and then take appropriate steps to avoid the same errors in the future.

Physicians and staff need to look out for the barriers that often prevent us from achieving our goals of service excellence. Ask staff what they perceive as barriers. From an operational standpoint, the organization can then move forward to reduce those barriers. Often, health care providers say they cannot provide a high level of excellence to patients because they don't have enough time. However, as pointed out in prior chapters, it is often not a matter of time, but rather a matter of the tone that they exhibit with patients.

✔ Policies and procedures

A part of creating a five-star practice means taking another look at systems and policies and procedures to make sure your quality improvement efforts are ongoing. This could mean incorporating policies that concern hiring, orientation, evaluations, and bonuses. It could mean reexamining policies and procedures on disclosing medical errors or adverse events. It can mean developing policies for reporting adverse events to patients under appropriate circumstances. It also may mean policies affecting safety, cross training, or telephone triage, as well as scheduling polices and procedures.

Delineating these examples highlights how moving to a five-star practice touches on many aspects of a health care organization. It means looking at the overall culture, i.e., the macro, but leadership as well, i.e., the micro. By evaluating the macro and micro, we truly provide the pervasive, concentrated, and continuous effort necessary to make service excellence part of the culture.

Patient Involvement and Accountability

It is important to make patients partners in their own care and accountable for their own health. Physicians should send patients the message that says, "I have certain responsibilities and obligations to you that I must live up to. However, so do you. If we both live up to our respective responsibilities and take care of your health together, you'll fare far better."

For many years we have acknowledged that patient behavior contributes to unfortunate or untoward results. They do not stop smoking, do not exercise, do not take their medications as prescribed, fail to show for follow-up visits, do not come in for their annual exams, or simply do not follow their physician's instructions. Yet when something goes wrong, patients often blame the physician. Why? In part, it is because they have never truly been held accountable for their own care. Of course, we need to do this in a positive, rather than adversarial, fashion.

Studies show that patients want to be involved in their care. This feeling has grown in recent years with patients taking time to obtain information about their illnesses and procedures via the Internet. So if they want to be involved in their own care, let's put them to work.

Of course, patient involvement doesn't happen just because you want it to. Think through what it means for your particular specialty, clinic, hospital, or practice. Encouraging patient involvement must be embedded in every step of your process. Every staff member should agree that patient involvement is an essential part of your collective goal.

Several positive outcomes result when we make patients our partners. For one, we can significantly reduce the likelihood of a professional liability claim and lower the severity if a claim moves forward. Patients are also more likely to comply if they acknowledge their responsibilities, and you document that acknowledgement. Patients who have a document that sets forth their responsibilities and the consequences of not complying will be reluctant to seek an attorney. If they do, the attorney will be less likely to accept their case.

To truly develop a partnership with the patient, there has to be a cultural change within your organization. Statements such as, "You are an important part of your health care team," should be prominently displayed. They should be woven into your marketing materials, patient brochures, Web site, and reception area bulletin boards. It has to become part of your discussions with the patient and the family.

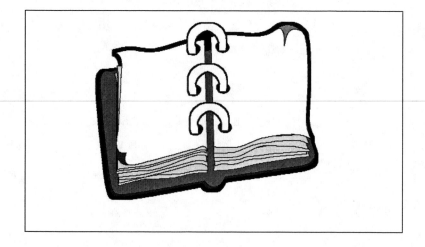

Admittedly, a cultural shift is tough to accomplish. It requires a commitment by all physicians to truly involve the patient. It means reviewing the way in which patients receive instructions, for example, and how care plans are developed. Are instructions easy to understand? Do we give patients tools to help them help themselves?

The tools could include something as simple as sending a postcard to remind patients that it is time to schedule their annual visit. The reception area in one West Coast dermatologist's office offers patients a pamphlet about the importance of regularly scheduled visits for skin disorders. The pamphlet gives recommended time intervals between appointments and describes what happens in cases of late diagnosis and how it changes the physician's ability to easily treat the skin condition. It also discusses how treatment becomes more invasive the longer it is put off, as well as the implications for patients who decide not to follow the doctor's instructions.

This pamphlet is an example of a tool for achieving greater levels of patient involvement. Some practices around the country have been far more innovative in using media such as the Internet, electronic monitoring, or telemonitoring. Elements of disease management also become applicable. The point is to look at your particular practice and patient population to determine which areas need significant levels of patient compliance and involvement. Once you target this group, review the tools you will use to accomplish this goal. Determine whether those tools are readable, easy to use, and clearly explain what the patient and/or patient's family should and should not do. If the tools are explicit in their instructions, you will begin to see a difference in patient compliance levels.

Turn your history form into
a liability risk reduction tool

Two easy steps

A few simple changes to your patient history form can boost your liability protection by making patients more accountable for their own care. Consider the following:

1. **Introductory sentence:** Place wording at the top of the form to remind patients of your reliance on them to provide complete and accurate health history information. For example: *"The following information is very important to your health. Please take the time to fully and accurately fill out this form."*

2. **Signature and date line:** Include a space to capture the patient's signature and the date at the end of the form. Follow with the phrase, *"I attest that the above information is true and correct to the best of my belief."* This emphasizes the important role that the patient plays in his or her own care.

These two simple features transform common history forms—often fraught with errors and omissions—into liability risk reduction tools.

History forms often don't include the patient's complete health history. For example, a nurse may not have required the patient to complete the entire form, perhaps assuming that the physician would go over it with the patient during the office visit. This kind of scenario often ends up in court years later, with the physician unable to recall the visit that took place so long ago. The patient, meanwhile, remembers the visit well and testifies that he or she did provide a complete account of his or her health history. This type of contest is easily avoided by following the steps outlined above.

In fact, there is anecdotal evidence that these changes actually make patients more thoughtful about the information they provide. Some physicians say patients have insisted on bringing the form home so that they could take time to fill it out completely.

Patient brochures

Many practices and facilities provide disease- or condition-specific informational brochures to communicate important topics to patients. These brochures set the stage for informed consent by including the following wording:

"This office takes informed consent very seriously. We will discuss options with you including surgical options. We will ask you to review a film.

You will then discuss your procedure with your surgeon and our nurse educator. We will make sure that all of your questions have been answered.

At the end of the educational process, we will ask you to accept responsibility for your treatment decision. Do not sign your informed consent form until you understand the risks and alternatives, and all of your questions have been answered. It is important to us that you fully understand this information."

A typical brochure describes the following:
- The patient and physician's responsibilities
- The physician's expectations of the patient
- The importance of providing complete medical history information and to notify the physician when their are changes in condition
- How patients can contact the office and why they may have to wait several hours for the physician to return their call
- Frequently asked questions
- Where patients can access additional information on their disease or condition
- Contraindications and risks associated with certain treatments or procedures

Some brochures include spaces in which patients can record their blood pressure, weight, important telephone numbers, instructions they have received, questions that they have asked, and the answers they have received. Of course, this information should also be placed in the patient's chart.

A patient brochure for obstetrics, for example, would include information about prenatal care, the birthing process, common complications that can arise, a description of common symptoms, changes that the patient should expect during different stages of her pregnancy, and other information that expecting parents need. It might also include a check-off sheet that the patient can mark whenever she attends Lamaze classes, for example, or receives additional information from the physician.

It is important for the physician to document that he or she has provided the patient with this information. Suppose the expectant mother is an insulin-dependent diabetic who risks developing preeclampsia after 26 weeks. The obstetrician provides her with several different informative sheets, tells her what symptoms to be wary of, and urges her to call if any of the symptoms occur. The physician does not document in the patient chart that the patient has received this information.

Later, the patient does become preeclamptic, yet does not call the physician's office. She has received so much information that she doesn't remember the specific instructions that the physician gave her regarding these dangerous symptoms. As a result, her situation turns critical, her complications are significant, and she suffers neurological damage from a seizure.

In the wake of this unfortunate result, the plaintiff's attorney tries to prove that there was a lack of education, coordination of information, and instruction on the physician's part. Guess which side the jury sympathizes with?

Providing a one-stop-shop brochure to patients—and documenting that you have done so—can help avoid this classic "he said, she said" courtroom contest.

Let's look at the brochure's usefulness from another angle. A continuous litigation problem over the years for obstetricians has been that of informed consent. Recall that informed consent is required in most jurisdictions for any operative or invasive procedure. Although the case law is mixed, some courts have ruled that informed consent would be necessary prior to per-forming an episiotomy or even using forceps. Even if informed consent is not strictly required in your particular jurisdiction, or it falls into a gray area, it is extremely important for patients to know when an episiotomy must be done and why an assisted delivery would be advisable for both mother and child.

However, the reality is that true informed consent is often difficult to acquire. The mother may be medicated during labor. Certainly both parents are anxious, excited, frightened, and often exhausted. These aren't ideal cir-cumstances for obtaining informed consent. However, if the obstetrician previously provided the parents with an informational brochure that fully discusses labor and delivery, and if he or she already discussed the possibility of an episiotomy and its inherent risks and complications, then the physician can refer back to the brochure during labor when explaining why an episioto-my has become necessary.

✓ **Think about your specialty and write down two major procedures or conditions for which you know patient compliance is an issue.** Then, apply the concepts discussed in this chapter. You will begin to see the areas in which you can improve upon your patient education efforts.

Because the parents have already read and signed off on the brochure and the information contained in it, they understand—even in the midst of labor—what an episiotomy entails and why it has become necessary. The physician has obtained true informed consent. If an adverse event does occur, a plaintiff's attorney will have a difficult time proving negligent conduct, let alone showing how the physician did not make the parents aware of all of the risks.

The brochure should be to the point and easy to understand. This is not just another piece of paper they are receiving; this is a document that they should use week in and week out. It should list pros and cons, explain the scenarios upon which certain decisions will have to be made, and invite questions. There should also be a place for a patient and witness signature.

Although the brochure does not take the place of informed consent, it can be treated in a similar fashion. An OB nurse, for example, should review the three standard informed consent questions to verify that the patient has read about the complications that can arise, such as assisted deliveries and episiotomies, understands what she has read, and has no questions. (See Chapter seven: Documentation: Creating a Net, p. 59.) This provides additional informed consent documentation. It also is a good process to ensure that the patient truly understands this important information actively involved in treatment.

When discussing this concept with obstetrical expert David B. Acker, MD, director of obstetrics of Brigham & Women's Hospital in Boston and associate professor of obstetrics at the Harvard Medical School, he explained there is certain information that the parents clearly need during the prenatal period to help them understand the labor and delivery process and to ensure a good or better outcome. Placing this important information, particularly in certain high-risk situations, in one document in a very readable fashion can have significant positive patient implications.

KEY

PROVIDING BROCHURES, DISCUSSING THE INFORMATION IN THEM WITH PATIENTS, AND ENCOURAGING PATIENTS TO PLAY AN ACTIVE ROLE IN THEIR OWN CARE IS KEY TO PROMOTING PATIENT SATISFACTION. IT CAN ALSO:

- IMPROVE OUTCOMES
- CONTROL YOUR LIABILITY RISK
- ENHANCE YOUR PRACTICE
- PLACE INFORMATION AT A PATIENT'S FINGERTIPS
- REDUCE THE NUMBER OF TELEPHONE CALLS FROM PATIENTS
- IMPROVE OUTCOMES
- REDUCE PATIENT ANXIETY
- INCREASE PATIENT COMPLIANCE

Creating a virtual school to educate patients

In orthopedic surgery, a frequently performed procedure is a total knee replacement. To teach patients about this procedure, some orthopedic practices actually send their patients to a virtual knee replacement school.

The "school" begins when patients arrive to discuss the procedure. They receive a brochure that explains the procedure and its risks, the various alternatives, rehab and follow-up care, how patients can impact their own recovery, and a check-off sheet for additional information they may review.

The school continues on each subsequent visit, when the surgeon literally works through the brochure with the patient. He or she checks off the conservative therapy the patient has attempted, for example, and notes that the patient wants to contemplate definitive surgery. He or she reviews risks and alternatives with the patient and checks that section off. The patient also views a videotape about the procedure.

When the patient has completed all of the components of the school, a nurse or the surgeon checks off the final box and both parties sign the brochure to confirm the patient's "graduation." The signature also indicates that the patient understands that conservative methods have not been successful, that he or she has been informed of and understands the risks and alternatives of total knee replacement, that all of the patient's questions have been answered, and that the patient knows what he or she needs to do postoperatively to help his or her own rehabilitation.

Surgeons who use this form of patient education report exceedingly high levels of patient satisfaction and better outcomes. When there is an unfortunate complication, the well-educated patient may not even consider going to an attorney. If he or she does, the attorney may be hard-pressed to accept the case, realizing that the patient has been so well imformed. If it prevents one claim, it is worth the time and the effort of putting a school program together.

The 'at-risk' letter

Every facility and practice has certain patients who put them at risk. These are the patients who do not follow instructions, fail to keep appointments, and are essentially noncompliant. If noncompliance becomes a critical issue, the patient should receive an at-risk letter. (See a sample letter, p. 57.)

The letter is usually sent to patients through certified mail to warn them that their noncompliance could have a serious negative effect on their health. It does not need to be lengthy, but should set forth the following:

- Specific areas in which the patient is noncompliant
- The risks of remaining noncompliant
- How the patient can get his or her care back on track
- A closing sentence indicating, in a positive manner, that the physician is counting on the patient to help achieve the desired result

Such a letter meets our dual goal of improving outcomes and care while reducing liability exposure. When asked why they do not comply, patients have provided the following answers during a trial or deposition:

- "I did not realize how serious it was."
- "I had no idea how important that test was."
- "Of course I would have followed the instruction, if I had only known."
- "They didn't tell me how important it was to keep my leg elevated."

We need to take these excuses away from patients and put the ball of responsibility squarely in their court. An at-risk letter accomplishes this.

A certain subset of patients will immediately comply upon reading such a letter and seeing the consequences of their noncompliance in print. It may be that they did not hear or fully understand your initial instructions to them. They may have heard you but quickly forgot what you said once they left your office and became busy with their day-to-day activities. No one wants a bad result, and when you tell these patients they are headed for one, they become motivated to take charge.

In some cases, loved ones may see the letter. They may open the family's mail and, upon seeing that their husband, wife, mother, father, or partner is not following instructions and putting him- or herself at risk, they become worried and help their loved one get back on track.

The letter should be firm and clear without being antagonistic. If carefully crafted, these letters can have an effect on the patient's ability to bring a claim if an adverse event does occur. The plaintiff's attorney, upon seeing this letter in the patient's chart, will know that he or she will have a much more difficult time proving malpractice or negligence than without it. If the case proceeds to the courtroom, this document will be blown up to the size of a movie screen to show how the complications were a direct result of the patient's noncompliance.

Health care professionals do a very good job when it comes to educating patients and coordinating care, but are far from where they should be when it comes to getting patients more invested in their own outcomes. This must be done under the umbrellas of patient satisfaction and service excellence.

Sample 'at-risk' letter

Send this letter to non-compliant patients and document that you did so.

Date

Dear [*insert patient's name*]:

It has come to my attention that you are not adhering to the medical regime that I have instructed you to follow. It is necessary for you to [*insert the advice, recommendation, or regime*] for important health reasons. If you fail to do so, it could have the following negative effects on your health: [*list consequences of not following treatment*].

We are committed to providing you with quality health care, but to do so, we must count on you to follow your prescribed treatment. You are a critical part of the health care team.

If you have any questions about what you must do, please call our office at [*insert phone number*].

Sincerely,

[*insert physician's name and signature*]

KEY

THIS LETTER IS A TOOL THAT PROMOTES HEALTHY OUT-COMES AND REDUCES THE POTENTIAL FOR COMPLICA-TIONS CAUSED BY NONCOMPLIANCE. IT ALSO LESSENS A PATIENT'S UNREASONABLE EXPECTATIONS WHILE PROVID-ING YOU WITH CLEAR DOCUMENTATION OF THE PATIENT'S NONCOMPLIANCE.

Documentation: Creating a Net

Good documentation has always been recognized as a way to reduce malpractice exposure. For years, health care professionals have heard that "if it is not documented, it was not done." Clear documentation reduces liability exposure in a number of ways. Good documentation can literally prevent medical errors and create a safer environment. Many articles have been written about mistakes due to illegible notes. Juries have awarded large sums in medical error cases that have resulted from a physician's sloppy handwriting.

There is little humor in jokes about physician's handwriting these days. Plaintiffs' attorneys look for poor handwriting. They look for a note that cannot be read and use technology to blow it up to the size of a movie screen in the courtroom. These attorneys ask jurors whether they can read the note and, when they can't, ask how the physician could have expected anyone to read it. They try to illustrate how sloppy documentation and messy handwriting is indicative of a messy and careless physician. (See the writing sample on p. 60.)

We must practice offensive, rather than defensive documentation. We should use it as a net to catch the excellent care we provide. Good documentation systems show that patients are well-informed and understand the critical role they play in their own recovery.

What a mess!

Jurors are unforgiving about lazy documentation, including sloppy handwriting. It brings up safety, liability, and regulatory considerations. It is time to start addressing it in a more serious way.

Often, physicians don't realize just how critical their handwriting is. It shouldn't take seeing your note from the medical record blown up on screen in the courtroom to develop better handwriting habits.

Plaintiffs' lawyers focus on documentation as an indication of the care being provided. Is it sloppy, disorganized, or rushed? This is infrequently the case, but you can see how, in front of a jury, this conclusion could be drawn.

Review your documentation regularly. When it is illegible, refer the problem to your medical staff process. It is a serious safety issue, and it is time to treat it that way. Case in point: To the right are notes taken from an actual patient file. One can only imagine a jury's reaction.

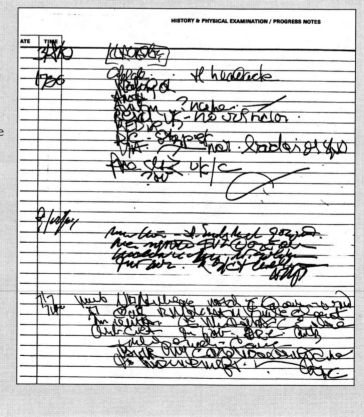

HISTORY & PHYSICAL EXAMINATION / PROGRESS NOTES

Take, for example, the case of an informed consent form and postoperative documentation that was used for an extremely difficult surgical procedure. A complication occurred during the procedure and, during the trial, the plaintiff's attorney alleged that there had been a lack of informed consent. Unfortunately, the informed consent form did not specify the procedure or the surgeon's name.

In the same chart, there were progress notes that set forth important facts about the patient's postoperative condition. This was critical information for the defense of the case. Unfortunately, the progress notes were illegible. The physician was most likely told about the importance of documentation during his residency, and probably sat through at least one risk management discussion about it, but to no avail. Now a major professional liability suit will hang over his head for years.

How much time would it have taken for the surgeon to include the name of the procedure on the informed consent form and to make sure that progress notes were legible? How much time would it have taken to document that he discussed all possible complications with the patient? The time it takes to accomplish these important goals is far less than the amount of time it takes to defend a malpractice claim.

The patient chart

The patient chart is a critical part of documentation. It must be clear, well-organized, easy to use, understandable, and include vital information to allow continuity of care. The history form included in the chart should require the patient's signature and stress the patient's responsibility for providing complete and accurate information, as described in Chapter Six (See "Turn your history form into a liability risk reduction tool," p. 48.) Everyone involved with the patient should be familiar with the chart and any new information that has been added to it.

Using a standardized method of documentation is important, particularly in a group practice. Most defense attorneys have sat through a deposition in which one member of a group could not decipher another's notes. Juries never forgive physicians with dangerously messy handwriting—or the colleagues who let them get away with it.

Check-off sheets

This is an extremely easy and inexpensive documentation strategy. Physicians give so much information to patients that it's hard to keep track of it all. In fact, they often hand out the information without documenting that they have done so. A simple check-off sheet in the patient chart can accomplish this. It allows you to document what information you provide to patients and when you provided it. Thus, when an issue arises and the patient says, "I don't believe I ever received that information," you can simply point to the checklist in the patient's chart to show that he or she did receive the information.

Sample: Check-off sheet

This example contains a sampling of various forms that may be included in an OB/GYN check-off sheet. Of course, each physician should create check-off sheets that include forms and brochures that address the specific needs of his or her patients.

[Name of practice/facility] Check-off sheet

Document	Date	Initials
Patient brochure		
Informed consent		
History sheet		
Illustration/explanation of surgery		
About your anesthesia		
Pre-op instructions		
Post-op instructions		
Description of disease processes and what to watch for		
Dietary restriction instructions		
Smoking		
What to expect during labor/delivery		
A month-by-month guide to care		
Diabetes management		
Exercise		
Anatomical illustrations		
Becoming a dad		
Baby care		
Your baby's first year		

Informed consent

Informed consent is the process of informing the patient about the risks of, and alternatives to, a specific procedure. To that end, various tools have been developed to aid in the process, including films, worksheets, and software programs.

The process of obtaining informed consent is often viewed as a burdensome legal process. Although this is perhaps true in some respects, informed consent should be regarded as a crucial educational and patient-involvement tool that encourages patients to accept certain responsibilities.

Done properly, informed consent can reduce the patient's expectations to a more manageable and realistic level. It can also reduce your liability risk by educating the patient and his or her family about the complications that can occur and about the importance of deciding whether the offered procedure is worth the risk. Nowadays, when disclosure of complications is mandated, informed consent can save the day. Remember, when a patient is told of a risk after it occurs, it is an excuse; when the patient is told of the risk before it occurs, it is part of the informed consent process.

A good informed consent process does not have to be time consuming. It can be integrated into patients' visits and can be aided by the nurse educator, physician assistant, or certified nurse practitioner. In fact, many practices use procedure-specific forms for their informed consent process, such as for spinal surgery, orthopedics, cardiac catheterization, or colonoscopy.

This is a document that not only educates the patient, but also reduces your liability risk. It can be created in collaboration with a hospital or surgery center or can be an office-based form. It typically does not change the process that is already in place. Also hold an inservice for the physicians and staff to review the form and emphasize its importance. (See sample form, page 65)

Sample: Informed consent to operation, treatment, and invasive procedure

It is very important to [*insert name of practice or organization*] that you understand and consent to the treatment your physician is rendering and any treatment your physician may perform. You should be involved in any and all decisions concerning surgical procedures that you will undergo. Sign this form only after you understand the procedure, its risks, its alternatives, the risks associated with the alternatives, and only if all of your questions have been answered. Please initial and date directly below this paragraph to indicate your understanding of this paragraph.

_____   _____
(Patient's initials or authorized individual)   (Date)

I, _____, hereby authorize Dr. _____
and any associates or assistants whom he or she deems appropriate, to perform

_____

upon   _____
          (Name of patient)

The physician has explained the benefits of the procedure(s) to me. I understand there is no certainty that I will achieve those benefits and that no guarantee has been made to me regarding the outcome of the procedure(s).

I authorize the administration of sedation and/or anesthesia as may be deemed advisable or necessary for my comfort, well-being, and safety.

The physician has explained to me that there are risks and possible undesirable consequences associated with this and any procedure, including, but not limited to: blood loss, transfusion reactions, infection, heart complications, blood clots, loss of or loss of use of a body part or other neurological injury, and/or death. I understand that if I need to receive blood or blood products, this will place me at risk for contracting HIV/AIDS, hepatitis, or other diseases.

In permitting my physician to perform the procedure(s), I understand that unforeseen conditions may be revealed that may necessitate a change in, or extension of, the original procedure(s), or a different procedure(s) than that/those already explained

---

(cont.) Sample: Informed consent to operation, treatment, and invasive procedure

to me. I therefore authorize and request that the above-named physician, and his/her assistants and designees, perform such procedure(s) as necessary and desirable in the exercise of his/her professional judgment.

The reasonable alternative(s) to the procedure(s) have been explained to me. These alternatives include *but are not limited to* _____

_____

I hereby authorize my physician to utilize or dispose of removed tissues, parts, or organs resulting from all procedure(s) authorized above.

I consent to any photographing or videotaping of the procedure(s) that may be performed, as long as my identity is not revealed by the pictures or by descriptive texts accompanying them. I also consent to the admittance of students or authorized equipment representatives to the procedure room for purposes of advancing medical education or obtaining important product information.

_____   _____   _____   _____
(Date)   (Time)   (Patient signature or   (Relationship of
                             signature of authorized   authorized individual)
                             individual)

☐ The patient/authorized individual has read this form or had it read to him/her.
☐ The patient/authorized individual states that he/she understands this information.
☐ The patient/authorized individual has no further questions.

_____   _____   _____
(Date)   (Time)   (Signature of witness)

Certification of physician
I hereby certify that I have discussed and explained the facts, and the risks associated with this and any alternative procedure(s) described in this consent form with the individual granting consent.

_____   _____   _____
(Date)   (Time)   (Signature of physician)

(cont.) Sample: Informed consent to operation, treatment, and invasive procedure

Use of interpreter or special assistance
An interpreter or special assistance was used to assist the above named patient in completing this form as follows:

☐ Foreign language (specify)
☐ Sign language
☐ Patient is blind/form read to patient
☐ Other (specify)

_____

Interpretation provided by:

_____
(Name of interpreter and title, or relationship to patient)

_____   _____   _____
(Date)   (Time)   (Signature of interpreter/individual
                            providing assistance)

Author's note: This should be used as an example of a general informed consent form only.

There are many variations, depending on whether informed consent is obtained in the hospital or practice setting. Many hospitals and practices have chosen to use procedure-specific informed consent forms. Legal requirements regarding informed consent vary among jurisdictions. Legal counsel should be consulted to ensure that all applicable legal requirements are satisfied in a particular informed consent form.

Give more responsibility to your informed consent 'witness'

Give the witness' role greater weight in the informed consent process. Historically, it appears that the witness' only role in the informed consent process was to witness the signatures.

However, witnesses should have a much greater responsibility. Specifically, the informed consent witness should verify that the patient read the form, understood it, and had all of his or her questions answered. This is important because the questions that the patient asks are usually what drive informed consent malpractice cases.

Consider the following scenario involving a patient who suffered a stroke during a surgical procedure:

Q *Mrs. Jones, is this your name at the witness line?*

A Yes it is.

Q *Mrs. Jones, could you explain to the jury what it means when you sign here as the witness.*

A Well, you see that there are several questions right on the form. It is my practice and in fact, my job, to go through those questions. I will only sign as a witness if in fact the patient responds "yes" to the first question (Have you read the form?), "yes" to the second question (Do you understand the form?), and "no" to the third question (Do you have any questions?).

Q *Mrs. Jones, I want you to look at the paragraph where it lists certain complications. Do you see it? I have it blown up on this poster board, which has been marked as defendant's Exhibit 8?*

A I see it.

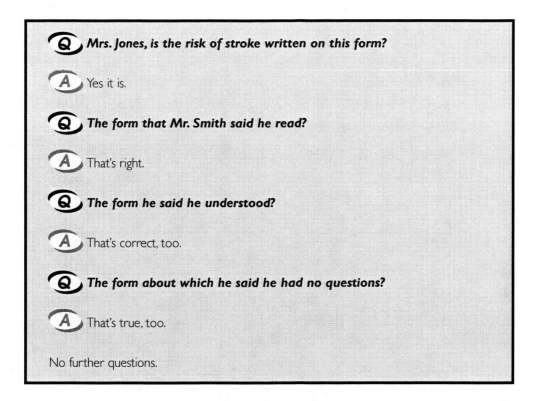

> **Q** *Mrs. Jones, is the risk of stroke written on this form?*
>
> **A** Yes it is.
>
> **Q** *The form that Mr. Smith said he read?*
>
> **A** That's right.
>
> **Q** *The form he said he understood?*
>
> **A** That's correct, too.
>
> **Q** *The form about which he said he had no questions?*
>
> **A** That's true, too.
>
> No further questions.

Graphic Surgery, LLC, recently developed an innovation in this area. Patricia Gelnar, MD, PhD, a trained neurosurgeon, and her partner, Carl Lauryssen, MD, developed a software program to aid the physician's informed consent process. The program, titled Doc-Tour System, has the potential for use by risk managers, health insurers, and others, but its primary goal is to educate the patient on the risks of and alternatives to surgery.

The patients view a virtual procedure on a computer at the physician's office. After, they can ask the physician questions. They are then given a password to access the virtual procedure from home, where they can view the procedure as many times as they would like. Seventy percent of patients who have received passwords have logged on to view the procedure from home.

Telephone interview with Patricia Gelnar, MD, PhD, of Graphic Surgery, LLC (April 14, 2003).

Informed refusal

A topic similar to informed consent that has been coming up more recently is that of informed refusal. This evolves from the noncompliant patient who simply will not accept a certain recommendation that you have made. This noncompliance can breed a lawsuit, particularly if the patient dies. For example, the shocked, grieving family may say their family member would never have refused treatment that would have extended his or her life. However, the family member isn't there to rebut that assertion.

A simple form can be created that describes the recommended treatment, the reason the treatment is needed, and the consequences of not having the treatment. Upon refusal, the patients signs the form. Family members may place pressure on the individual, but everyone will be on the same page as to who is making the decision and who is responsible.

Sample: Informed refusal of test, procedure, or treatment

My physician, _____, has recommended the

following test/procedure/treatment:

_____

_____

He/she has explained to me that the potential benefits of the test/procedure/treatment

include:

_____

_____

and that the risks are:

_____

_____

Despite my physician's recommendation, I refuse to consent to this medical treatment.
The physician has explained the following risks to my refusal. They include, but are not
limited to:

_____

_____

By signing this document, I acknowledge that my medical condition has been evaluated
and explained to me by my physician, who has recommended treatment as stated
above, and that the doctor has explained to me the potential benefits of such treatment and the risks associated with it, as well as the probable risks of not following
the recommended treatment, which I fully understand. In spite of this understanding,
I refuse to consent to this medical treatment.

_____   _____   _____   _____
(Date)   (Time)   (Patient signature or   (Relationship of
                           signature of authorized   authorized individual)
                           individual)

☐ The patient/authorized individual has read this form or had it read to him or her.
☐ The patient/authorized individual states that he or she understands this information.
☐ The patient/authorized individual has no further questions.

_____   _____   _____
(Date)   (Time)   (Signature of witness)

The patient chart

Time and again in the courtroom, there are subtle and sometimes not so subtle suggestions that the way someone completes their documentation is a reflection of the care they provide. Is it thoughtful, organized, legible, and understandable? Or is it haphazard, disorganized, and hurried? The chart needs to be well-organized so information is easy to find and understand.

Although this sounds like common sense, there are several cases each year in which illegible writing is the issue. Consider the following quotes, taken from depositions:

- "You just don't understand how little time we have, compared with the number of patients we see."
- "The only person who needs to know what's being done with the patient knows how to read my handwriting."
- "I've written like this for 20 years and nothing bad has ever happened."

Telephone triage form

It is easy to think that a call is routine and not significant. But patient calls must be documented as a matter of habit. When a mother calls a pediatrician to describe the progression of her three-year-old child's symptoms, for example, the physician must determine whether the mother should bring her child in that night or the next morning, or whether he or she should prescribe a certain medication.

Every year, defendants are hurt by their own inability to document conversations properly. They may exchange clinical information over the phone with a patient but don't document it clearly in the patient's chart—or at all. Here's where a telephone triage pad can help. This is simply a pad with preprinted areas to capture important information, such as the date and time of the call, the patient's name, and the physician's responses to the patient's questions and concerns. Place these pads next to all telephones, and ask physicians to carry them in a pocket. (See example below.)

Telephone triage form

This could be developed into a pad that the doctor puts into his or her coat pocket, or it could be kept at home or in the car. The note could be inserted into the chart as is or transcribed at a later date. We must do more to capture information communicated during telephone calls.

PATIENT NAME: _____

PHYSICIAN: _____

DATE: _____   **TIME:** _____

PATIENT'S QUESTIONS/CONCERNS: _____

_____

PHYSICIAN'S RESPONSE: _____

_____

The discharge letter: A last resort

You may have experienced the following scenario: The physician has been working hard to keep the patient on a certain treatment regime, but the patient has missed visits, taken his or her medications sporadically, gone off his or her diet, and appears to be headed for a bad medical result. Other times, the patient is rude with staff and unappreciative, no matter what the staff try. The situation gets to a point where the physician and staff have simply had enough.

If you find yourself in this situation, always try to rectify the relationship first. Discharge should only be used as a last resort. There will always be difficult patients in your practice, but only a few will be deserving of this rather drastic step. Thus, warnings ought to be placed in the chart exemplifying that discussions have taken place, and that the patient has been informed that his or her behavior is unacceptable. Make sure your instructions to the patient are specific and understood, and that the implications of not following them have been carefully reviewed.

If these efforts fail and it does become necessary to "fire" the patient via a formal discharge letter, write the first draft and send it to your legal counsel. This will allow you to vent your feelings—and allow your lawyer to make edits to an often highly emotional letter.

The discharge letter should set forth the following in a nonaccusatory and very factual style:

- The reason for discharge
- A statement affirming that the patient's behavior is unacceptable and that the patient has been counseled about this before

- An offer to see the patient for emergent reasons over the next 30 days only
- A statement urging the patient to seek a new physician within 30 days and to request transfer of his or her records to that physician

The letter should be sent via certified mail with return receipt requested. It should discuss how the physician-patient relationship can impact the patient's health/recovery and that the physician has chosen to terminate their relationship due to the patient's continued lack of compliance. The letter should suggest that the patient take time to find another practitioner with whom he or she can develop a more positive relationship and provide a phone number to call for information about physicians of similar specialties. The letter should also stress the therapeutic importance of finding another physician as quickly as possible. Finally, it should express regret that the physician-patient relationship has come to this conclusion but that you feel it is in the patient's best interest to find a physician with whom he or she can develop a close, effective, and positive relationship.

Again, this letter should not be written in an angry tone, but in a very factual fashion so it will not come across as spiteful or vindictive if read later by a jury. If it is eventually read by a jury, the letter should leave jurors with the impression that the physician truly was trying to help the patient.

Be prepared to provide records promptly to the patient's new physician and do what you can to make the transition smooth. Do not speak to other health care professionals or to the patient's new physician about the patient's behavior. (See sample termination letter, p. 76.)

Sample patient termination letter

Date: [insert date]

Dear [insert patient's name]:

This letter is to inform you that I will no longer be your physician and will stop providing medical care to you effective [insert a date that is 30 days from the date of this letter].

It has come to our attention that you have failed to show at your last several scheduled appointments. This is not withstanding the fact that our office has sent you [insert number] written reminders. Our office views the physician-patient relationship as critical to our goal to provide you with appropriate and safe care. It is clear to us that we have been unable to create that relationship with you and therefore must terminate the relationship at this point in time.

We will continue to provide emergency care to you for the next 30 days while you seek another physician. However, we expect a letter requesting transfer of your records to another provider within the next 30 days. There are many fine family practitioners in our community, and if you need any help finding a suitable physician, please do not hesitate to contact [insert name and telephone number of an appropriate referral source].

We regret that this step is necessary, but feel it will be in your best long-term interest. We do hope you will find a physician with whom you develop the type of trusting relationship that enables you to feel comfortable and follow through with your treatment plan.
Sincerely,

[insert physician's name and signature]

A few additional points about discharge

Patients do not like to be fired. They may try to argue their way back into the practice. Usually, this is because they want to be the one who makes this ultimate decision. Sometimes they truly want to return to the practice because your staff put up with their abusive behavior and they're not sure that other health care professionals will. Some worry that it will have a negative impact on their ability to obtain future health care services.

Regardless of the reason, once your decision is made, stick with it. History has taught us that even the most contrite patient is likely to continue the same disruptive behavior. In a few instances, patients have successfully reincorporated into a practice when the physician and staff draw up a tightly written "care contract" with the patient. The contract sets forth the change in behavior or compliance that must take place and what will happen if it does not.

Recognizing When You Are At Risk

Let's pretend for a moment that you are the receptionist who has the very important duty of greeting patients. You have gone through service excellence programs, so you know those first 10 seconds are critical, and you really want to make them count. A new patient walks in and you look up. You make eye contact, offer a big smile, and then you are suddenly struck by something unusual about his forehead.

As he moves closer you see that it is a bright red tattoo. The tattoo reads, "I will probably sue you!" The man is pleasant enough and gives no outward appearance of hostility, but you can't get your mind off the tattoo. Having received such a blatant warning, you will most likely treat this patient differently than others. You may even quickly explain that the practice is closed and that there are other practices that may be far better for him!

Unfortunately, patients don't walk around with bright red tattoos stating their intentions (although we might prefer that they did), but they *do* exhibit red-flag behaviors. Learn to recognize them, because there are things we can do to avoid the imaginary tattoo's prophecy.

Many physicians say they don't have time in their busy schedules to hand-hold needy patients, even if they do exhibit red-flag behavior. But this doesn't have to be the case. You can develop strategies for dealing with these patients. After all, the tone that you take with patients leaves more of an impression than the amount of time you spend with them.

Some facilities and practices schedule high-maintenance patients with a physician assistant or nurse practitioner with strong communication skills and longer blocks of time. This does not mean that you are dumping difficult patients on to your advanced practice caregivers; it simply means that when certain patients need more communication and explanation, perhaps a different type of caregiver is necessary for that purpose.

Further, many physicians have discovered the benefits of spending quality time with patients. They strike that balance between not being rushed and not permitting their schedule to be crunched. For example, they ask open-ended

questions early on in the appointment rather than waiting for the last
30 or 40 seconds. They make eye contact, stay on time, and avoid looking at
their watch.

In these ways, you can reduce your exposure to lawsuits and patient dissatisfaction without overburdening your schedule. Having additional educational
materials, adjuncts to the way in which you provide information, ready-made
question-and-answer sheets, or videos, e-mail, and group visits will help
provide the level of communication that your patients need.

KEY

LEARN TO REALIZE WHEN YOU ARE AT RISK WITH A
PATIENT AND DO SOMETHING ABOUT IT. PHYSICIANS
AND NURSING STAFF OFTEN SUBCONSCIOUSLY DO
THE OPPOSITE. IF A PATIENT IS UNPLEASANT, THE PHYSI-
CIAN AND STAFF MAY RUSH TO GET THROUGH
THE VISIT. HOWEVER, FROM A RISK
MANAGEMENT STANDPOINT, YOU SHOULD GIVE YOUR
UNPLEASANT PATIENTS THE SAME 110% THAT YOU GIVE
TO EVERYONE ELSE. IT MAY TAKE MORE EFFORT TO DO
SO, BUT IT IS FAR BETTER THAN GIVING THIS PATIENT
THE IMPRESSION OF DISINTEREST, OR EVEN RUDENESS.

Red-flag warning signs

About 15% of your patients create 85% of your risk. No doubt, this 15% is a tough bunch! The following can help you determine who these patients are and under what circumstances you should be wary:

- **Patients who complain about their past health care provider.** Are you going to be next?
- **Patients who have chronic physical, psychological, or emotional problems.** These individuals are high-maintenance, so pay a little more attention to them than to the average patient. But consider this time well spent.
- **Patients who do not understand their care or the information that you communicate to them.** Perhaps there is a language or a cultural barrier, or the patient has a mental impairment. Patients who do not understand will likely leave your office feeling disappointed and unsatisfied. They can be harsh with you on patient satisfaction surveys and criticize you to the community at large. Thus, part of your goal should be to increase their level of understanding by encouraging their involvement and accountability.
- **Patients who don't listen to what you say.** Sometimes a patient's schedule is just as busy as the physician's. These patients are often two steps ahead of themselves and are always thinking about the next thing that they have to do, so they may not truly listen when you give them important information or instructions. Other times, you may have a casual relationship with a patient who may say, " Doc, you don't need to go through all that stuff with me. Just fix my knee so I can get back on the slopes." Beware: Every patient should have all complete information to provide a true informed consent. Take the time to explain the importance of the latter. Review the risks of the procedure and witness the informed consent signature to make sure the patient reads the form, understands it, and has no further questions.

You begin to see how these principles work together to significantly reduce your liability exposure. That is why the goals described in this book are so important and so effective: We are going to the heart of what causes dissatisfaction, frequency of claims, and severity.

Event Management

Now let's put some of your good work to use. As mentioned in previous chapters, incorporating certain proactive principles into your practice will not only help prevent lawsuits, but also the threat of a lawsuit. And although the best risk management activities won't prevent all claims, proactive measures will greatly enhance your defense during a trial and can bring a more favorable resolution.

When you receive a letter, phone call, or visit from an unhappy patient who threatens to sue, you will feel a combination of emotions, including panic, anger, embarrassment, and perhaps some fear. In part, this is because you are now in unchartered waters. This contact may come long after your treatment has ceased. You may not recall the specific circumstances surrounding the patient's procedure or medical regime. You will become defensive. You may even contemplate a countersuit. Your mind works full steam ahead.

If you do receive such notification, the first thing you should do is slow down. You do not have enough information to make good decisions about the next steps, and your swirling emotions can cloud your good judgment. In fact, this visit, letter, or phone call does not have to lead to a lawsuit. Sometimes it is merely a cry for help from the patient.

If something has gone wrong, this is your opportunity to derail a lawsuit or reduce the severity or value of what may be a real claim.

Perhaps the patient does not understand why he or she did not receive a desired treatment. Perhaps the patient died and a family member is calling because there was not enough communication about why death occurred. Maybe the patient keeps receiving an invoice for a matter he or she believes has already been settled. You must take steps to diffuse the patient's anger, as this is your last attempt to prevent a claim and a golden opportunity to create documentation and interactions that can strengthen your case if the claim moves forward.

The first hours following an event are critical as to what direction the family or patient may go. Sometimes you may not even know an event has occurred. Regardless, your behavior immediately following an event or allegations of one is critically important. In fact, plaintiffs' attorneys around the country say they pay close attention to physician and office staff conduct. A lack of disclosure, for example, or a lack of communication after an event has occurred makes the case more appealing to them.

Suppose you receive a letter from a patient complaining about a course of treatment. First, examine the patient's chart and review what took place. Then speak to your professional liability insurer or your facility's attorney to help you plan your course of action. He or she will suggest that you look at the issue from the patient's point of view so you do not become too defensive when speaking to the patient. This is crucial because any statements you make to the patient can be used against you.

Meet with your risk manager or attorney to craft a response letter to the patient. The letter can be used as evidence in a lawsuit, so it should be thoughtfully and carefully written. Your response should be timely. Nothing makes patients—or jurors—angrier than to be ignored when a complication has occurred.

The plaintiffs' attorneys are able to orchestrate a very realistic and emotional scene. For example, Mom went in for an elective procedure. The family was barely aware of it, since Mom has always been a fairly private person and keeps most things to herself. The informed consent process was benign, given that the procedure was not risky.

Unfortunately, a complication occurred and Mom is now in the intensive care unit. Family members must travel long distances to see her. One daughter literally travels all night. When they arrive, they demand to speak with the physician. They want answers. This is not surprising conduct, given their stress, lack of sleep, fear, and perhaps guilt.

If the family is unable to receive the information they feel they need, or if they perceive the physician as evasive or unresponsive, they will become more frustrated and angry. These feelings will be burned into their recollections. It is therefore best to respond to these early warning signs with tact, compassion, and patience. This type of event management should be mandatory.

Event management is a tremendously underutilized tool. Perhaps it seems counterintuitive. In the difficult professional insurance liability marketplace, health care professionals have been reluctant to seek advice from their insurance carriers when something goes wrong. However, that is exactly what you should do. Disclosure of medical errors has become an important concept and is certainly a growing trend. Studies have shown that when disclosure of an adverse event or a medical error occurs it actually reduces the potential of a claim and even the severity of that claim if one is ever asserted. Plaintiffs' lawyers have begun to use a lack of disclosure or the lack of good communication to their advantage.

True event management requires you to develop policies and procedures for investigating adverse events and near-misses. You must look for true, objective facts by asking why something happened. Meanwhile, you should keep the patient and his or her family informed about your investigation into the incident, since lack of information is the leading reason why patients and their families seek an attorney. It's useful to provide the family with a contact person at your hospital or organization who can answer their questions.

This process will support your efforts toward continuous quality improvement. After investigating an event, your performance improvement team should assess clinical and service weaknesses, with a strong focus on identifying communication deficiencies. You can then develop employee education programs to strengthen those weaknesses. Thus, event management can halt or reduce the severity of a lawsuit, inspire caregivers collaborate, and promote your performance improvement efforts.

KEY

THOUGHTFUL RESPONSES, LETTERS, AND MEETINGS CAN STOP LAWSUITS. THERE ARE MANY ANECDOTAL STORIES IN WHICH THE PHYSICIAN TOOK TIME WITH THE PATIENT, APOLOGIZED, AND ENDED UP NOT BEING NAMED IN A LAWSUIT THAT WAS FILED AGAINST OTHERS. REMEMBER THAT THE DYNAMICS HAVE CHANGED AND INFORMATION IS NOW MORE IMPORTANT THAN EVER. COORDINATE YOUR RISK MANAGEMENT AND EVENT MANAGEMENT STRATEGIES WITH OTHERS, INCLUDING YOUR RISK MANAGER, BUSINESS MANAGER, INSURER, OR PRACTICE ATTORNEY.

Pretrial Preparations

The most frightening thing about the litigation process is the unknown. And although litigation is certainly a process that health care professionals hope they will never encounter, it is actually something that many will have to face at some point. Understanding what the process entails will help you see the critical importance of the prevention strategies outlined in this book and why it is essential for you to partner with your facility's organization's attorney.

Too often when a lawsuit is filed, the physician takes a hands-off position. He or she may simply respond, "I'll let my attorney handle this. This is why I have liability insurance." The attorney cannot handle it, however, without the physician's help. A physician's conduct and active involvement in the case can greatly enhance the result.

For this reason, this and the following chapter contain an overview of the litigation process. The process differs from jurisdiction to jurisdiction and depends on whether the lawsuit is filed in state or federal court. However, you can generally expect the process to resemble the following:

Initial stages

The patient will send legal papers—either a writ of summons or an actual complaint setting forth allegations of negligence—to your professional liability insurance carrier or risk manager.

The complaint is often a frustrating document to read. Remember that it is simply the plaintiff's allegations. Although the law requires a good-faith basis for each of the allegations, a complaint often includes every conceivable claim, it's perceived cause, every conceivable type of damage.

Here are some strategies for responding to a complaint:

1. **Secure the chart.** Remove nothing from it and make no changes to it. This may seem like an overly obvious suggestion, but well-meaning practitioners have often been tempted to simply "make the chart more accurate" by inserting notations that they are sure were said or done. This happens infrequently, but when it does, it is disastrous to the defense.

2. **Set up a separate file for your legal documents.** This file can become very thick. Do not mix your legal documents, such as letters between you and your attorney, with the medical chart. There have been cases in which the chart has been copied by a practice and sent to a plaintiff's attorney, and it contains certain correspondence between the physician and his or her attorney.

3. **Do not speak about the case to colleagues or anyone involved in the care of the patient.** These conversations are not protected or confidential. Except in peer review setting or in a discussion with your attorney, there is no such thing as an off-the-record conversation.

4. **Meet with your attorney to discuss every aspect of the case before drafting a response.** Your attorney needs to have a deep understanding of your case. You will review the medical records with him or her, walk through your care of the patient or the procedure performed, and explain your diagnosis and your critical thinking leading up to the diagnosis.

5. **Respond to the complaint.** This is an important process, so your attorney must have a thorough understanding of the facts and the medicine involved in order to file an appropriate answer. This is the first brick in the foundation of your defense, and erroneous answers to the complaint can come back to haunt you later. Unless the complaint is legally deficient, an answer must be filed. If the complaint is legally deficient, your attorney may decide to file a preliminary objection. This can take different forms, depending on whether you are in state or federal court. A preliminary objection may mean that portions of the complaint seek damages that are not permissible or appropriate under the circumstances and should be stricken. Legal briefs need to be filed to support the objections, and the court will rule on them before the matter can move forward.

Discovery: Uncovering the facts

The idea behind discovery is to make each side familiar with the other's case. When all the information is known, fair evaluations can be made. The thought is to prevent undue surprise and promote settlement of the claim, if appropriate.

Chapter Ten

Often a plaintiff serves certain discovery, such as a "Request for Production of Documents" or a request to answer "interrogatories," with the complaint. These two forms of discovery request documents and information in your possession that are pertinent to the plaintiff's case.

Unless they have already obtained it, the plaintiff's attorney will want the patient's chart and any other relevant records you may have. He or she may ask for statements you made, corporate documents, your policies or procedures, and your applications for staff privileges at hospitals or health maintenance organizations. Your attorney should review this request to ensure that no legally protected information, such as peer review information, has been requested. If so, a timely objection to the production of that information must be made.

Interrogatories will include queries into your background, training, experience, practice, and relationships with your professional corporation or managed care organizations, and will carefully probe your care of the patient. You may be asked about continuing legal education, journals you subscribe to, and textbooks you have in your office. Again, some of these questions may be objectionable, and your attorney may object within a specified time frame. When little information is provided in response to a request, the plaintiff may file a motion with the court demanding more complete answers. Your attorney will request similar information from the plaintiff.

Make sure you carefully review your responses to the discovery request, particularly the interrogatories. If you have questions about it, ask your counsel to explain why something was or was not stated. If there are inaccuracies, clarify them before this becomes a final document. After all, no one knows the facts better than you do. Your attorney may have misinterpreted something you said during your initial meeting, and it will be difficult for you to contradict this kind of discrepancy later on. Besides, contradicting your response will make you appear unreliable and will be used by the plaintiff's experts to support their own opinions.

Depositions

The purpose of the deposition is generally two-fold:

1. **It is part of the discovery process.** The attorney conducting the deposition collects facts upon which he or she will build the case.

2. **It helps build a factual foundation for your case.** Your expert witness will use this to opine about the care that was rendered. Attorneys for both sides will collect facts in a fashion this is most helpful to their clients. Often, attorneys will craft questions so that the answers will be more favorable to their particular case. This is why you cannot simply go into a deposition expecting to merely explain what happened and everything will be fine. The process is intensely adversarial. Each attorney attempts to do the best job possible for his or her client.

Depositions are one of the most important parts of your case. In the deposition process, each side may take the oral testimony of the plaintiff and the defendant, as well as all factual witnesses, and in many jurisdictions, expert witnesses. Attorneys representing all parties are present, and a court reporter puts the individual to be deposed under oath and records the proceeding. In most jurisdictions, the involved parties have a right to be present, although that seldom occurs. You may want to be present for such depositions and should discuss this with your counsel.

There is a great deal of strategy involved in how, when, and why depositions are taken. Most attorneys are very cautious to make sure all pertinent facts involved in their case are completely uncovered. In most cases, the majority of those who have rendered care and whose names are on the chart will be deposed. This may include prior and current treaters, the pathologist, the radiologist who interpreted diagnostic tests, nurses, physical therapists, and hospital risk managers. On the plaintiff's side, it could include family members, employers, or friends who were listed as witnesses.

Any individual who is deposed should be represented by an attorney during the deposition. If your receptionist and office nurse is deposed, your attorney can and should represent their interests. Subsequent treating physicians should contact their professional liability carrier and ask them to provide counsel. This protects the deponent When the deposition of an expert witness is allowed, your attorney may want your guidance in understanding medical issues and the nuances of the medicine in the case. As always, preparation is crucial.

The three legs of credibility

Your overall goal throughout your deposition should be to maintain your credibility. This is the most important element of your case, since ultimately these cases boil down to whom the jury believes.

Many cases focus on one fact that can influence the outcome of the entire case, such as whether the standard of care was met, although opinions about this fact are often based on very different understandings and beliefs about what happened. You'll use three legs of credibility to stand on during your deposition and trial: your confidence, your word choice, and your defense team.

Your confidence will result from solid preparation with your attorney. Your word choice helps establish credibility while your body language helps build it. For example, responding with a confident "yes" or "no" is more powerful than, "usually I would not," or "I think so." Your credibility is solidified the experts you choose, the attorney you have, and the way your case is prepared and presented.

Your deposition

In your deposition, you have an opportunity to amplify certain portions of the record and articulate your thinking. You will also be able to discuss your reasoning, which will help your experts understand and support your case.

Unfortunately, it also allows the plaintiff's attorney to assess your demeanor and credibility. Poor performance during your deposition could be a determining factor in how you are used as a witness during trial. If it is determined that you are not going to give credible testimony on your own behalf the plaintiff's attorney may decide to call you early on for cross-examination. A poor job during your deposition could also drive up the value of the case, which may be important if you determine that it should be settled. Correspondingly, a strong performance at your deposition can have the reverse effect on all accounts.

All depositions are important, but none compare to your deposition in a professional liability claim. Potentially, this is an opportunity to dispose of the matter before going to trial. Through your deposition, the plaintiff's attorney may see that the claim is without merit, or because of your testimony, the plaintiff's attorney may not find expert support for the theory set forth in the complaint, and the case may have to be dropped. An earlier expert evaluation has probably already taken place by the plaintiff, but a final report is not prepared until after the deposition.

What you say can be used against you

Your testimony during your deposition could be used directly in court. Generally, your deposition is transcribed by a court reporter and perhaps recorded on video-tape. During trial, portions of your testimony may be read or viewed by the jury. If you give testimony in court that is inconsistent with your deposition, the plaintiff's attorney will question your credibility by showing how you have tried to change your testimony. Consider the following example:

A patient is unable to produce a urine sample during an office visit, so the physician tells the patient to come in the next day to try again. The physician testifies during her deposition that she did not know whether the patient was told of the impor-tance of bringing in the urine sample the next day—meaning that she does not have a *specific recollection* of telling him to do so.

During the physician's pretrial preparations, however, it becomes clear that she made it her practice to impress upon all patients the importance of following up on all diagnostic exams, and that her nurse always reminds patients about it on their way out the door. In retrospect, her testimony during the deposition was the result of fatigue and nervousness, rather than dishonesty. (Continued on next page)

During the trial, the physician and her attorney realize this is an important point and that the physician should have spelled it out when asked about it. Her testimony at trial goes as follows:

Q *Doctor, you don't really know whether you told the patient about the importance of bringing his urine sample in the next day, since he couldn't produce one at your office. Isn't that right?*

A Well actually that's not right. I do impress upon them the fact that it's important that they follow up with their test and, in fact, my nurse reminds them on their way out. (Plaintiff's attorney pauses, with a surprised look, then reaches for a copy of the physician's deposition transcript from a file.)

Q *Doctor, let me hand you a copy of your deposition transcript, taken in my office three years ago. Do you recall that proceeding?*

A I recall it.

Q *Just so the jury understands that process: You came to my office with your attorney, right?*

A Yes.

Q *And can we assume you told the truth on that particular day?*

A Of course I did.

Q *All right, and if I could just take a minute to read my initial instructions to you which I think you will recall. Reading from page three, on that day I explained to you, "Doctor, please, when I ask a question, make sure you understand the question and don't answer until you do." Do you recall me asking that?*

A If it's in the transcript, I'm sure you did. I do not remember exactly.

Q *And after your deposition, you were sent a copy of your deposition transcript and an errata sheet and had the opportunity to review the deposition and sign that it was accurate or make any changes. Isn't that right?*

A Well, I remember getting it and I did review it.

Q *Doctor, right here on the errata sheet you signed indicating that you had reviewed the deposition and that it was a correct recording of the deposition, right?*

A Yes. That is my signature.

Q *So this is a document that represents several hours of questions and answers between us from over three years ago, specifically about this case. Isn't that right?*

A Yes, I guess that's true.

Q *Certainly these questions came at a time much closer to the actual events than now. We can assume your recollection would therefore be better.*

A That's obvious.

Q *And I recall from your deposition that you said you had an opportunity to review all the records and prepare for the deposition and even meet with your attorney, right?*

A Well, yes.

Q *So you came to your deposition prepared to give testimony about the facts in this case, you were represented by counsel, you were put under oath, you understood that everything was being taken down, you had an opportunity to review the transcript, and you signed it. Is that a fair summary of what has taken place?*

A Well, all that is true.

Q *Now, let me draw your attention to page 178 of your deposition. (Witness complies.) I asked you a question similar to what I just asked you here in court. I asked you, "Did you impress upon the patient the importance of bringing a urine sample in the next day?" Do you see that question? Did I just read it correctly?*

A Yes, I see it.

Q *At that time, under oath, after being prepared to give your deposition, you said, "I do not remember if I did." Isn't that what you said?*

A That's what the deposition transcript states, but . . .

Q *Well, doctor, that's not only what the deposition transcript states, that's actually what your answer was as recorded by the court reporter, isn't that right?*

A Well, if you put it that way.

Q *Now doctor, three years later, here in the courtroom, I just asked that exact same question and you gave a different answer, didn't you?*

A No, well maybe. Well, yes.

Preparing for the deposition

Preparation is the key to a good deposition. A complete and thorough understanding of all the facts is essential. You need to know where the plaintiff's case is coming from and where your defenses will take you. Your deposition preparation should be a process and not just one meeting.

Spend time with your attorney so you understand the plaintiff's theme as well as your own. Without understanding themes, you will hear questions and not realize how they are connected. This type of understanding can only be accomplished when you and your attorney brainstorm where the plaintiff's case is going and have a complete understanding of the clinical issues of the case.

Make sure you have all the documents you need and that they are well organized. Your documents should include the complaint, your answer to the complaint, the answers to interrogatories that you have responded to, medical records, and a recent copy of your curriculum vitae.

> **To prepare, you need a thorough understanding of :**
> 1. The facts
> 2. The plaintiff's position or theme
> 3. Your own position or theme
> 4. All clinical issues and supporting literature
> 5. All clinical records
> 6. All documents filed, including the complaint, the answer to the complaint, the answer to interrogatories, and responses to the requests for documents or admissions
> 7. The legal process
> 8. The plaintiff's attorney
> 9. The setting
> 10. The kinds of questions that will be asked

Have your attorney review what he or she thinks will be the key issues in your case. Your attorney will also have an expert witness examine the case for potential weaknesses. It might not be that the treatment or medicine provided was weak, but that the documentation is unclear. Ask about the plaintiff's attorney who will be questioning you and find out what type of questions he or she will ask. Your attorney should prepare you by asking sample questions or going through a mock deposition with you.

The process

Frequently, the plaintiff's attorney will begin the deposition giving you instructions. Generally, the instructions will be similar to the following:

Good morning, Dr. Smith. My name is Sally Sharp. I represent the plaintiff in this case, which has been initiated against you and Dr. Jones due to medical treatment that took place in 1999 and shortly thereafter. This is my opportunity to ask you questions concerning care and treatment and to get your responses, which will be recorded here by the court reporter. I would like to keep this informal, and I don't expect it to run very long. So relax, and we'll get started.

There are some important instructions. Please remember that I'm not trying to trick you; if you don't understand a question, let me know, and I will repeat it or rephrase it. If you need to review the chart prior to answering a question or would like to check with your attorney before answering, let me know and we'll give you an opportunity to do that. Make sure your response to the question is verbal, since the court reporter cannot take down a nod of the head.

These instructions seem simple, but they are important. Once I ask you a question and you respond, I'm going to assume that you heard and understood the question, that your answer is your complete answer, and that it is truthful. Fair enough? Okay then, let's proceed.

The instructions seem innocuous, but a lot of things are taking place. Attorneys will try to make the process seem straightforward, sometimes even casual—but do not let your guard down. Depositions are inherently adversarial. As the previous example shows, within these instructions is language that can hurt you at a later time if you give testimony that is at odds with your deposition. So listen carefully and provide your full attention and concentration.

Typically, the attorney will begin with detailed questions about your background, education, and training. I recommend bringing an up-to-date copy of your curriculum vitae to help the process run more smoothly. Because your anxiety will be high, it will be easier to remember the dates in question with the document in front of you. Be prepared to talk about your schooling, internship, residency, employment status, employment history, training, board certification, certification exams, board certification, and the scope of your training and experience. Often questions are also asked about literature you have contributed to or programs you have completed. Other questions may focus on professors with whom you have worked. Sometimes they even ask those professors to be an expert against you.

The attorney will want to know about specific training as it applies to the case. For example, if you are questioned in a case involving an infection, the amount of course work and clinical practice you had in that area will be covered in detail. If the case is about a certain surgical procedure, be prepared to discuss how many you have performed and the results of each. Prepare yourself to talk about every aspect of your background by talking to your attorney about how these details will fit into your case. The key is to explain that you have the appropriate background, training, and experience to perform the procedure in question or render the type of treatment at issue.

Your role in your own practice will be discussed, including the organization of your professional corporation or your employment circumstances. If you have left a practice in the past, this will be discussed even though it appears as though your privacy is being invaded. This is discovery, after all, and judges interpret the rules of discovery very liberally.

After your credentials have been thoroughly reviewed, the flow often turns to abstract questions concerning the clinical issues involved. If the case is about an infection, perhaps the questions will focus on signs and symptoms of certain types of infections and the tests that could be used to determine their presence. The questions may focus on the types of treatments available and about the efficacy of those treatments.

There may be questions about studies or literature that exists about the condition or treatment in question. This does not mean that you need to memorize the world's literature pertaining to your treatment. However, you should have a working knowledge of the medical issues and understand how these issues fit into your case. For example, the blanket statement that the more promptly cancer can be treated, the better the outcome, may not apply to your particular case. If your case involves a delayed cancer diagnosis, expect to be asked about the significance of delay in treatment or diagnosis.

Sometimes a single statement from a textbook may be used out of context. You and your attorney will need to ask for an opportunity to review whatever is being read to you if a textbook or journal is being used. You will want to make sure it is read in context and then answer the question in context. Often plaintiff's attorneys will come in with a stack of journals and textbooks or chapters from texts. Sometimes this is done to intimidate. These articles and text chapters often will be the basis for many questions, so pay careful attention to them. Never agree with a snippet of information that is read out of context.

Chapter Ten

Once there is a thorough discussion of your background and clinical issues related to the standard of care, causation, and damages, the deposition will turn to your treatment in this case. It is imperative that you have a complete working knowledge of all medical records involved. If your treatment took place in the hospital, you should assemble the hospital record and review your progress notes, orders, laboratory results and, when they were available, nurses' and consultants' notes. Put the record together chronologically. There is usually a great deal of ammunition in the record to show that tasks were accomplished and appropriate care was given.

If the case involves only your office treatment, you must understand not only your records, but the records of your partners who may have seen the patient, any tests you received, a review of the telephone log if you have one, and a review of your billing records. Make sure you understand all the notations in the record.

Once you have a thorough understanding of all the notes and records in the chart and how they fit together, you need to understand how the plaintiff's attorney will ask questions about them.

Deciphering unruly documentation

The time to decipher one of your partner's notes is not at your deposition. Jurors are not forgiving of physicians who cannot read their partners' notes. This is becoming more of an issue as multispecialty groups and larger practices become more common. In the future, you may have new partners or be involved in networks, resulting in more people than ever on your team. Consider the following example from a malpractice case:

Q *Doctor, would you agree with me that continuity of care is very important to the patient?*

A Of course it is. I stated that earlier in my deposition.

Q *I remember. Further in that regard, I assume it is going to be important for you to have an understanding of not only what the patient's symptoms were when you saw the patient, but what they were historically—perhaps several days before?*

A That's true.

Q *That's the reason you keep a medical record, in part, isn't it? So that you will have the ability to see what a prior physician may have done as well as what his or her thinking was, the result of the clinical exam, correct?*

A That's true. We also speak to each other and discuss patient care issues, of course.

Q *But certainly there are times when other physicians aren't available to speak to you, which is the reason we need to set forth the information in the medical record.*

A (Several moments later) That's true.

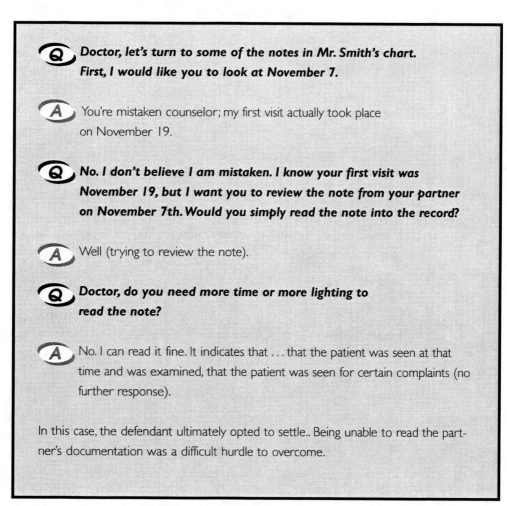

Q *Doctor, let's turn to some of the notes in Mr. Smith's chart. First, I would like you to look at November 7.*

A You're mistaken counselor; my first visit actually took place on November 19.

Q *No. I don't believe I am mistaken. I know your first visit was November 19, but I want you to review the note from your partner on November 7th. Would you simply read the note into the record?*

A Well (trying to review the note).

Q *Doctor, do you need more time or more lighting to read the note?*

A No. I can read it fine. It indicates that . . . that the patient was seen at that time and was examined, that the patient was seen for certain complaints (no further response).

In this case, the defendant ultimately opted to settle.. Being unable to read the partner's documentation was a difficult hurdle to overcome.

Questions to expect

Generally, there are two types of questions. One is an open-ended question asking you for a narrative of what took place on a certain date, such as, "Doctor, you first saw Mr. Smith on November 22, 1995. Can you explain to us the circumstances surrounding that visit and what took place?"

Open-ended questions give you an opportunity to provide your side of the story. Generally, you should answer these questions as simply as possible. Get right to the point without offering unsolicited information. With appropriate preparation, this can be effective. It is strategic in nature and should be discussed with your counsel.

The second type of question is a leading question. These questions suggest a certain answer, but leave little room for explanation. Consider the following:

 Doctor, you first saw the patient on November 12, 1995. Isn't that correct?

 That's right.

 And, looking at your record, it appears that the patient recounted to you that he experienced tightness in his chest and overall aching the day before, isn't that right?

 That's what the record states.

 Now doctor, as we discussed previously, you have an EKG machine in your office that you're qualified to operate, correct?

 Yes.

 You told us this machine was in the other room from where you were examining Mr. Smith that morning, isn't that right?

 Yes it was.

You testified that you are competent to use this machine and interpret the readings, isn't that right?

 That's true, but . . .

 And you agree that it isn't an invasive or difficult procedure, right?

 No, it's not invasive.

 In fact, it's actually a simple procedure to perform, isn't that right?

 That's true.

 Yet, the information you can glean from an EKG can be helpful in determining whether the patient has had or was having some type of myocardial infarction, right?

 It can provide helpful information.

 So you had this diagnostic test, which wasn't painful, invasive, or cumbersome. It could have yielded important information to you, and it was in the other room from this patient who was at risk for a heart attack and was complaining of symptoms consistent with a heart attack?

 Is that a question?

Q *Calling these statements questions is a bit of a stretch, but they are typical. There is a way to stymie a leading question, however, by using a more "correct" answer. For example:*

Doctor, is it a fact that the patient had chest pain, which you testified earlier can be associated with a myocardial infarction?

A No, what I said earlier was that chest pain can be indicative of myocardial infarction, but his pain was significant in being noncardiac in nature.

This provides a more correct answer—one that the plaintiff's attorney doesn't want you to give.

Thus knowing the attorney's style can be helpful in preparing for the deposition. Your attorney should tell you about the plaintiff's attorney and the style that he or she uses.

Does he or she cull information from textbooks and incorporate it into questions? Does he or she try to browbeat witnesses or try to lull witnesses into a false sense of security? Does the attorney normally proceed in an organized or a haphazard fashion? Is the attorney known for long depositions that take all day? Does the attorney use a lot of theatrics and exhibits during trial? The more you know about the process, the more comfortable you will feel and the more prepared you will be.

Chapter Ten

The following are several other forms of deposition questions that can be problematic to your defense if you are not familiar with them:

- **Repetitive questions:** Attorneys sometimes ask the same question several different ways in an effort to illicit a conflicting response from you. Repetitive questions can occur one after another or several hours apart. A sharp attorney will object to them if they have already been asked and answered. Otherwise, you can provide repetitive responses, such as, "Like I stated before . . . "

- **Summary questions:** An example would be, "Let me try to understand what you're saying; I guess it would be fair to say that you saw Mr. Jones on November 12, and you didn't think an updated history was necessary because you had seen him a few weeks before."

What you had actually said was that an updated history was not necessary since the patient had completed a history form on his previous visit, and the receptionist asked him for an update when he came to the office. The two statements are different, but when the plaintiff's attorney asks you whether it would be a fair statement, your tendency may be to agree if it is close. But beware any time the opposing attorney indicates that he or she is trying to help you by summarizing your own testimony. This is rarely the kind of help that you need.

- **Hostile questions:** When the response to a question is not what the attorney wanted, his or her demeanor may suddenly become hostile. Often this takes a witness by surprise, and the witness tends to agree with the statement the second time it is asked. Remember, the question did not change. The hostility or theatrics should be ignored. Remain firm in your responses.

- **Questions that refer back to scientific literature:** This can be problematic during a deposition. The attorney may have information from literature and may attempt to get agreement on medical themes. As reviewed previously, you have a right to look at the text or journal to which they are referring, to make sure the statement is not taken out of context—and you should do so. Follow your attorney's lead. He or she may place objections if an appropriate foundation has not been laid. Further, in some jurisdictions there is legal significance to admitting that a certain text is authoritative, meaning you agree with everything in it, which is rarely the case. Discuss with your attorney how to handle questions in your jurisdiction about textbooks and journals.

- **After-thought questions:** These are questions that relate back to an area of questioning that may have occurred perhaps a half-hour ago. Often the attorney will say, "Oh, I had one other question concerning the first visit," and then will ask it in summary form. Take your time answering. Get back to the point of reference he or she is asking about. It is easy to agree with the summary statement, but often it deals with a point the attorney was unable to make earlier.

- **Theatrics:** The plaintiff's attorney will watch your body language carefully, so it is important to maintain a professional demeanor. It is equally important to disregard the body language of the plaintiff's attorney, such as rolling of the eyes, raised eyebrows, or other indications of displeasure. This is done to intimidate you, so ignore it.

Don't let your guard down

It is tempting to relax once the deposition is completed, and conversation often begins to take on a casual tone. However, this can be a trap. When the deposition is completed, you and your attorney should leave. Too often, comments can lead to additional information being communicated. At the conclusion of one deposition, a defendant was heard to say, "I stayed up half the night studying some texts on infectious diseases, and she didn't even touch that area." This resulted in the deposition being re-opened.

Interacting with the plaintiff's attorney

Again, your demeanor is important. Be prepared, confident, compassionate, and knowledgeable. Listen to questions carefully and do not respond until you fully understand each one. When questions refer to a document, ask to review the document. If the question refers to a certain note in the chart, ask to review the note. Give your response in a straightforward fashion, using action words. As mentioned, a deposition is no place for "I think," or "usually." When you recall telling the patient the risks of a procedure, communicate that in your answer by saying, "I discussed the risk of infection during this procedure with the patient," rather than, "I usually tell my patients about the risk of infection."

If you are asked whether you recall a patient or treatment, and you do, say so with conviction. Often plaintiffs' attorneys ask such questions as, "Do you have a specific recollection of this patient, four years later, given the fact that you have a very busy practice and you've had thousands of patient encounters since then?" What the attorney is really asking is, "Do you remember?" Your recollection is important because it builds credibility. Be definitive and confident in your answers.

The cross-examination of a witness or a deposition generally lasts as long as you let it. In other words, if you leave cracks in your testimony, the plaintiff's attorney will try to split them open and lengthen the examination. However if you are prepared and definitive, the attorney will try to get things over with quickly.

The Trial:
The Ultimate Anxiety

Time and again, health care professionals say their trial was the most stressful and frightening experience of their lives. Physicians and nurses, like most professionals, are accustomed to being in control. Enduring a trial without having any real control over the outcome is incredibly stressful.

The more you know about the trial process, the more comfortable you will be. Set aside time to prepare yourself mentally and emotionally for this ordeal. Reducing the unknown is the key. Understand the progression of witnesses, receive a description of the court personnel, and perhaps tour the courtroom ahead of time so you will be familiar with its layout. Following is a brief description of the process.

Voir dire

The trial begins with voir dire, the process by which jurors are chosen. The number of jurors chosen will depend on whether you are in state or federal court. The way the voir dire is conducted also depends on the jurisdiction. Generally, the process begins with a large panel of potential jurors. The judge asks them general questions about their knowledge of the case and whether they personally know any of the attorneys/parties involved. At this stage, the judge tries to determine whether there is any reason why an individual cannot serve as an impartial juror.

Once the judge completes his or her questioning, the attorneys usually pose their own questions to the potential jurors. Because the plaintiff bears the burden of proof at trial, the plaintiff's attorney is allowed to ask his or her questions first. This is a very strategic time for the attorneys because it is where they warm up the jury with a first impression of their style and evidence.

A particularly important question for potential jurors is whether they have had a conflict with a health care provider that has left hard feelings. Asked the right way, this question can glean important information from jurors who have an underlying bias against health care providers. One such juror who cannot set aside his or her own bias can adversely affect the entire jury. Thus, some potential jurors can be stricken for cause if they appear to be unable to remain impartial.

Each side also may use "preemptory challenges" to strike several jurors. With the preemptory challenge, a juror can be struck for any reason. The resulting panel consists of 12 jurors and two alternates. Once the jury is selected, they are sworn in and placed in the jury box. A lot of science and style go into choosing a jury. Some attorneys even employ consultants to help with this process. The key strategy is to find jurors who do not have a bias and build rapport and credibility with them.

Your involvement with voir dire

You should discuss your involvement in voir dire with your attorney. Ideally, juror lists should be reviewed with your attorney before selection so you can plan a strategy. Be careful that jurors don't get the impression that you are picking over or prejudging them. However, if you see, feel, or detect a potential problem, let your attorney know in a subtle manner, perhaps by passing a quick note to him or her. But remember, the prospective jurors will be watching you. You are the main attraction.

Opening statements

Once the trial is underway, attorneys from both sides will summarize their case to the jury in an opening statement. This can be a defining moment of the trial; jurors sometimes make decisions based on opening statements.

Usually because the plaintiff has the burden of proof, the plaintiffs' attorney will go first, followed by your attorney. Each opening lasts about 25 to 40 minutes, depending on the complexity of the case. Sometimes the court puts time limits on them.

Openings are hard on the health care professional. The plaintiff's claims of negligence and malpractice are being aired in open court. If the case involves a plaintiff who has been severely injured, openings can be emotional. However, the opening is really your first opportunity to see clearly where the plaintiff plans to go with the case.

The plaintiff's case

Following the opening statements, the plaintiff presents his or her case. In order to satisfy the burden of proof, a plaintiff calls witnesses to testify. For malpractice, a plaintiff must produce an expert who is familiar with the standard of care applicable to the case, and who can explain how it was breached. They must also have expert testimony indicating that the breach in standard of care was a substantial factor in causing the harm.

The way an attorney decides to strategically present a case depends on several factors. However, the plaintiff's case often begins with testimony from the patient, who recounts his or her ordeal in an emotional and detailed fashion. Other witnesses may include family members or friends who witnessed the patient's condition, and other physicians who have treated the patient. The plaintiff may even call you to the stand for cross-examination. This has special legal significance and can damage your case, since the plaintiff can examine you using questions you may not expect. Your attorney will prepare you carefully for this.

Next, the plaintiff usually calls his or her expert witnesses. For example, in an alleged misdiagnosis of breast cancer, the experts may include a family practitioner, an oncologist, and a general surgeon with training in oncology. Depending on the evidentiary rules and the jurisdiction, all could testify about the standard of care and causation if they can show they have sufficient familiarity with those particular issues.

Of course, your attorney will cross-examine each of these expert witnesses. Cross-examination is an extremely important part of the trial process. Studies have shown that jurors pay close attention to cross-examination, since they feel this is the opportunity for the opposing attorney to really test the strength of the testimony they have just heard.

Your demeanor while the plaintiff's case is being presented is essential. This will be a tough and emotional time for you, since you are going to hear allegations about your care and treatment in court and in public. The plaintiff's expert could be vicious. Maintain your composure at all times, because the jury will study your reactions for insight regarding how you feel about these allegations—but this doesn't mean that you should remain stone-faced, either.

Contain your comments both in and out of the courtroom. Civil jurors are usually not sequestered—they go home each night and return each morning. They could be behind you on the sidewalk, in the elevator with you, or across the way at lunchtime. In one case, a juror commented after a verdict that he was very upset with the physician on trial because he felt that the physician did not take the process seriously. The juror said he saw the physician after court one day with a colleague, laughing it up. As it turned out, the physician's laughter and conversation had nothing to do with the case and was simply a release of nervous energy. Unfortunately, this juror misinterpreted it. Talk to your attorney about where and when it is appropriate for you to discuss the case and be especially conscious of your own conduct.

Your case

You will feel a great sense of relief once you are finally able to present your case. You have endured the allegations about your treatment, and now you have an opportunity to explain your actions. The jury should be looking forward to hearing your side of the story.

Rehearse your testimony completely beforehand, but not to the point of memorization, since there must be spontaneity to it so you appear real to the jury. Generally, your attorney will ask you some general questions to show the jury that you are a competent and well-rounded person—that you are well-trained, involved in the community, involved with your family, stay current in your field through continuing education, and that you have the appropriate training and experience to perform the treatment in question.

Next, your attorney may discuss your role in the case and how you became involved. This will lead to questions about your recollection of what occurred.

Your attorney will review each of the allegations made by the plaintiff's experts, and the jury wants to hear you refute them. All of the work you have done to establish and display your credibility boils down to this moment. Why should the jury believe your word over the patient's? The more you understand the process and the better you understand the goals of your direct examination, the easier it will be to provide your testimony.

After your testimony, you may call additional witnesses, which may include nurses in your office, colleagues, and concurrent or subsequent treaters. You will also call experts on your own behalf. If the pretrial preparation work has been done with the expert, this can be a rewarding time for you. Hearing a highly credentialed expert explain that your treatment was appropriate and exceeded the standard of care can provide a tremendous sense of relief to you while being very persuasive to the jury.

A cautionary remark is necessary here: Your anxiety may be high, and you may feel your expert witness has really saved the day, but you must remain as objective and detached as possible. For example, one physician was so pleased with the expert's testimony, he stood up and gave the expert a high five as the expert walked out of the courtroom. This was certainly the wrong impression to give to the jury. The physician realized this immediately, but it was too late. Although it did not affect the case, this is a scenario that keeps trial attorneys awake at night.

Closings

Once all the evidence is in, each side will present a closing statement. The closing is a critical part of the trial. All the evidence is now in. Both sides have been able to rebut certain testimony. Now, each side must put all of the evidence together and argue to the jury why they should prevail. Your attorney will spend long hours preparing this closing. He or she must anticipate part of the plaintiff's closing and make some comments to deflect the reasoning. The closing should lead the jury to the conclusion that the plaintiff did not meet the burden of proof and that malpractice did not occur.

The closings will be hard for you, as well. There will be points you want to make and times you want to stand up when the plaintiff's attorney is giving his or her closing to say, "That's out of context, that's not what the expert said." It can be infuriating, but you need to realize that the jury understands this is an adversarial process and that the plaintiff is focusing on the evidence that best supports their case—not yours.

Jury charge

Once the closings are complete, the judge will give his or her charge to the jury during which he or she explains the rules of evidence and the law that applies to your case. This can be a long, cumbersome, and complex process. Jurors try hard to listen, but they are learning difficult concepts in a very short time. The judge's charge, depending on the complexity of the case, could last from 45 minutes to an hour or more. The judge may also weave a discussion of the facts into his or her charge.

After the charge, the jury deliberates. At this point, you may have a sense of how the case went, but it is not over until the jury comes back with a verdict. The jury may return with questions—for example, in one case the jury came back seven separate times during three days of deliberations with questions about the evidence. Each question led to speculation about what the jury was thinking, but no conclusion could be drawn. To make matters worse, at the end of the third day of deliberation, the jury announced that it was hopelessly deadlocked, and the panel was dismissed. The whole trial was rescheduled and the process began all over again.

Such a case is rare, however. Judges generally ask jurors to attempt to reconcile their differences and come to a conclusion, but sometimes they cannot do so. If that occurs, the jury is dismissed, and a new jury is chosen for the case.

Chapter Eleven

When a jury does return with a verdict, it is yet another high anxiety time for you. Everyone stares at the jurors, wondering what they have decided. Many judges still follow the old school when it comes to reading a verdict. They ask the foreperson whether the jury has reached a verdict. The foreperson indicates that they have, and then the judge asks one of the court personnel to retrieve the verdict slip and bring it to the bench. After reviewing it, the judge becomes as stone-faced as the jury. Finally, the foreperson reads the verdict.

The conclusion of the case is welcome by all involved. However, the victory party is often cut short by news that there will be an appeal. Depending on your jurisdiction, this could be another lengthy period of litigation hanging over your head. Your attorney will explain the appeal time periods for your jurisdiction.

Once you have been through a trial, you will see why risk managers preach about principles such as documentation, appropriate policies, procedures, and informed consent. If you have good documentation and you have followed your policies and procedures, you will reap the benefit during your cross-examination. The plaintiff's attorney will use any conflicting statements you made during your deposition to damage your credibility. He or she will also try to discredit you by pointing out any omissions in your charts and documentation.

You can expect to be drained. Emotions run the entire spectrum but relief most of all. One point for sure, you will not want to be there again. This emphasizes the importance of proactive risk management principles. However, it should not take a trial to come to that conclusion.

Conclusion

We now have more insight into the reasons why patients file malpractice claims and juries sometimes award large sums to the plaintiff. It is time to use this information to reduce the chance that a claim will be filed in the first place and, if one is filed, to strengthen our defense against it.

Once we understand what can go wrong, how it goes wrong, and how it might be recounted in court, we can develop solutions. Moreover, we can greatly impact whether patients sue and, if they do, whether they will be able to put a strong case together.

The trick is to execute these solutions in your organization, *before something goes wrong,* since carefully planned and implemented risk management measures can significantly reduce your liability exposure. Incorporating the risk management principles discussed in this book can prevent nearly 60% of all claims. Every day we can take action to minimize the evidence that a potential a jury may one day weigh against us. Preventing even one claim makes all the time and effort you put into this process worthwhile.

We must turn away from defensive medicine and go on the offensive in a manner that enhances the physician-patient relationship. Understanding this is the first step toward protecting ourselves. The fact that these principles are also good for your practice and patients makes all of your efforts worthwhile.